PRESENTS

THE
GRIDIRON'S
GREATEST
QUARTERBACKS

JONATHAN RAND

www.SportsPublishingLLC.com

PUBLISHER: PETER L. BANNON

SENIOR MANAGING EDITOR: SUSAN M. MOYER

ACQUISITIONS EDITOR: BOB SNODGRASS

DEVELOPMENTAL EDITOR: KIPP A. WILFONG

ART DIRECTOR: K. JEFFREY HIGGERSON

SENIOR GRAPHIC DESIGNER: KENNETH J. O'BRIEN

COVER DESIGNER: JOSEPH T. BRUMLEVE

PHOTO EDITOR: ERIN LINDEN-LEVY

VICE PRESIDENT OF SALES AND MARKETING: KEVIN KING

MEDIA AND PROMOTIONS MANAGERS: SCOTT RAUGUTH (REGIONAL),
RANDY FOUTS (NATIONAL), MAUREY WILLIAMSON (PRINT)

Printed in the United States

ISBN: 1-58261-322-2

Sports Publishing L.L.C.
804 North Neil Street
Champaign, IL 61820

Phone: 1-877-424-2665
Fax: 217-363-2073
www.SportsPublishingLLC.com

Riddell®

RIDDELL® is a trademark of RIDMARK, INC.
used by permission.
Thanks to Hakan & Associates, the exclusive licensing agency for Riddell, Inc.

CONTENTS

CONTENTS

ACKNOWLEDGMENTS

When acquisitions editor Bob Snodgrass conceived our previous book, *Riddell Presents The Gridiron's Greatest Linebackers*, he was asked why we didn't start our "greatest" series with quarterbacks.

Well, here are the quarterbacks, and I'd like to thank those who graciously took time out for interviews. They include Sammy Baugh, Terry Bradshaw, Dan Marino, Roger Staubach, Bart Starr, Steve Young, Dan Fouts, Sonny Jurgensen, Y.A. Tittle, Len Dawson and Warren Moon.

I also want to thank those former NFL players, coaches and executives who graciously shed light on the careers of some of these 25 exceptional players. I was privileged to share the wonderful recollections of Don Shula, Marv Levy, Joe Schmidt, Bill Curry, Raymond Berry and Gil Brandt. Harvey Greene, Miami Dolphins senior vice president of media relations, provided valuable help.

I could not undertake any pro football history project without the help of the Pro Football Hall of Fame library staff, headed by Chad Reese. Nor without the help of Joe Horrigan, the Hall's vice president for communications.

I want to thank Bob Snodgrass of Sports Publishing L.L.C. for forging ahead with the quarterbacks book and Riddell, Inc., for its sponsorship. My enthusiasm for this project was boosted when I was assigned again to unflappable editor Kipp Wilfong.

This book was painlessly completed because my wife, Barbara Shelly, and son, Steven, made sure I had enough time and space. My older children, David and Danielle, spurred me on with constant encouragement.

Everybody knows a great quarterback when they see one. Or do they?

Joe Montana, rated in this book as the best quarterback of all time, was a third-round draft choice. Bart Starr, who led the Green Bay Packers to five NFL championships, was a 17th-round pick. Warren Moon, one of the most productive passers ever, wasn't taken in the NFL draft. And there are many other rags-to-riches stories.

There are, to be sure, such stars as John Elway, Terry Bradshaw and Troy Aikman whose talent was easy to spot. They were the top prizes of their drafts and won Super Bowls. Yet there's clearly more to a great quarterback than meets the eye. The job description could fill volumes.

"I don't think the job has ever been created that is more difficult than being a quarterback in the NFL," Hall of Famer Sonny Jurgensen said.

"It requires more time, work and dedication than any other profession I know. Its demands are both physical and mental. If there's a weakness anywhere in the quarterback's preparation, he lets down not only himself but his teammates, coaches and fans. The pressures are simply overwhelming, especially today when the entire NFL schedule is televised and with the possible financial implications of each game. It takes a special kind of person to really make it as a successful NFL quarterback."

Quarterbacks are special athletes, though those in this book vary widely in size, raw talent and temperament. Some were brawny and some were slight. Some had powerful arms and others merely accurate ones. Some were tortoises and some were hares. Some were choir boys and some were playboys.

All usually could find a way to win. All had unusual competitiveness, leadership and toughness.

Because quarterbacks are the glamour boys of pro football, it's easy to overlook the beatings they absorb. They get hit on most pass plays and there's no bigger trophy for a defense than knocking a quarterback out of a game.

Joe Namath, Dan Marino and Ken Stabler persevered on damaged knees. Staubach, Aikman and Young retired prematurely because of concussions. A dazed and bloodied Y.A. Tittle is the subject of one of pro football's most famous photographs. No wonder that former center Bill Curry quickly brings up toughness when he recalls the special qualities of Starr and Unitas.

"You couldn't keep them from going out there until you darn near killed them," Curry said. "They did leave games but only when something was torn or broken. All those things added up to them being two of the great leaders. I know I'm the luckiest guy in the world to have hiked the ball to both guys."

Old-timers will tell you it's become more difficult for a quarterback to lead effectively since coaches took away their play-calling duties.

"So often when you talk to players in the huddle, you're motivating them," Jurgensen said. "When you ask a receiver, 'Can you beat them to the corner?', you're putting him on the spot in front of everybody. Or when you say, 'Can you block this guy? We need a first down.' You're using psychology in leadership to get it done and you can't do that when a play's coming in from the sideline."

Jurgensen, a longtime Redskins radio announcer, isn't shy about challenging NFL coaches on this issue. He explains: "Coaches say, 'The reason we call the plays is we can scout the play as it's being executed. We know what play was called. We know why it breaks down or why it's successful. So it gives us a better feel and better control of the game. If you call the play, we don't know what you called until after the play.

"I say, 'We can change that. We'll let the quarterback signal the play to the sideline.' They don't like that too much."

Jurgensen spent his first four years as Norm Van Brocklin's understudy in Philadelphia, but a good young quarterback seldom sits long anymore. A team needs to evaluate him quickly because he's got a huge signing bonus and can become a free agent down the road. Any first-round quarterback these days probably will start as a rookie.

If a quarterback is patiently developed these days, he's usually a late bloomer or a coach once made a big mistake. Rags-to-riches passers such as Kurt Warner or Jake Delhomme started in Super Bowls after they bounced around the NFL and paid their dues in lesser leagues. They were groomed the old-fashioned way, but mainly by accident.

Recycled quarterbacks keep getting chances because there are nearly 100 quarterback jobs in the NFL and not nearly enough talent to capably fill them. Most teams have enough trouble finding a reliable starter, much less a second- or third-teamer.

Coaches with a quarterback problem often try to de-emphasize the position and ask their quarterback to play safe, mistake-free football. This can work if the defense and running game are sound enough. It doesn't work often.

Some experts have been quick to point to Trent Dilfer at Baltimore, Brad Johnson at Tampa Bay and Tom Brady at New England as evidence that it no longer takes a franchise quarterback to win a Super Bowl. There is, admittedly, no one formula for winning a Super Bowl, just as there's no one profile for an all-time great quarterback.

Rest assured, though, any coach would prefer trying to win a Super Bowl with a franchise quarterback. And, by the way, just because Brady was a sixth-round pick doesn't mean he's not a franchise quarterback. Just ask Montana, Starr or Moon.

When it comes to ranking quarterbacks, the number of championships won is the first criterion. And there is no second criterion. That's what most NFL coaches, executives, players and other experts will tell you. Unless, of course, they happen to be a quarterback, or an advocate for one, who's never won a championship.

Yes, championships are my number-one criterion for ranking the top 25 quarterbacks of all time. Quarterbacks are the ultimate impact players. When a franchise drafts a blue-chip quarterback, it expects him to produce a championship team. Few prospects at any other position generate such optimism.

But there are other criteria for great quarterbacks. They include statistics, games won, division and conference titles won and historical importance. Passing and rushing statistics are listed for regular-season games only, unless otherwise indicated.

Starting with Joe Montana, 18 quarterbacks in this book have led their teams to victories in Super Bowls or NFL championship games. Four others started in at least one Super Bowl or NFL championship game.

But if only Super Bowl winners were ranked here, Dan Marino and Fran Tarkenton would be among those out and Jim Plunkett and Tom Brady would be in. If Hall of Famers automatically made the top 25, Bob Waterfield and George Blanda would be in and Ken Stabler would be out.

Waterfield played just eight seasons and routinely was platooned. Blanda was an excellent quarterback but probably wouldn't be in Canton were it not for his kicking and longevity.

If only 3,000-yard passers were on my list, all-time greats Sammy Baugh, Sid Luckman and Bart Starr would be out and dozens of run-of-the-mill players could be in.

Despite all the statistics available to define quarterbacks, intangibles still matter. The best quarterbacks make smart, fast decisions and epitomize leadership and toughness. They stage dramatic comebacks by making 10 other players believe the unlikeliest victories are just around the corner.

Even some quarterbacks with great skills and intangibles fall short of a championship. Sonny Jurgensen seldom had a decent defense. Dan Marino usually went without a dominating running game or defense. For all of John Elway's talent and success, he didn't win a Super Bowl until 2,000-yard rusher Terrell Davis came along.

Because football is the ultimate team sport, greatness at any position is partly the result of being in the right place at the right time. San Francisco 49ers coach Bill Walsh suggested Montana might have wound up in Canada were he drafted by an NFL team that didn't correctly use his mobility and possession passing. And where would Elway have been if the hapless Colts refused to trade him after the 1983 draft?

Len Dawson had the misfortune to play five years for coaches who wouldn't let him off the bench and finally the good fortune to play for Hank Stram, who believed in him. Would Terry Bradshaw have won four Super Bowls had he not played for one of the most star-studded teams in NFL history?

Because luck is where preparation meets opportunity, I won't downgrade Montana or Bradshaw for making the most of a favorable situation. Nor will I penalize a quarterback for being a dominant figure in a less sophisticated era or a smaller league.

Otto Graham and Bobby Layne won NFL titles in a 12-team league. But it also took a terrific quarterback to start for most teams then. Even future Hall of Famers, such as John Unitas and Dawson, were released or stuck on the bench.

Baugh and Luckman, it could be argued, did not have to master today's complex passing schemes or face sophisticated defenses. Perhaps not, but how would today's quarterbacks like dodging a pass rush without the protection of a facemask?

Some current quarterbacks, most notably Peyton Manning, might be added to this list a decade from now. But as of this writing, Brett Favre's the only active passer who belongs. If you were judging greatness on the basis of an undefined career, Kurt Warner would have been on your list before he declined almost as rapidly as he had skyrocketed.

You might, of course, say the same of Joe Namath. But he showed tremendous talent and won a Super Bowl before his battered knees diminished his career. He also changed the history of professional football and that, too, is greatness.

With all due respect to your personal favorites who are missing, here's my ranking of pro football's 25 greatest quarterbacks of all time.

1. JOE MONTANA

Only one of two quarterbacks to win four Super Bowls, nobody elevated a team more than did Montana. For most of his career he threw to such marquee players as Jerry Rice, John Taylor and Roger Craig, yet won his first Super Bowl with a mostly undistinguished supporting cast.

In 1981, Montana had one top-flight wide receiver, Dwight Clark, and a mediocre running game. Montana led the 49ers to a dramatic victory over the Cowboys in the NFC championship game and a Super Bowl victory over the Cincinnati Bengals. It's hard to imagine any other quarterback leading those 49ers to a championship.

When surrounded by stars, Montana blew opponents away, as he did in Super Bowl wins over the Miami Dolphins and Denver Broncos. His comeback win against the Bengals in the January 1989 Super Bowl showed more Montana magic.

2. OTTO GRAHAM

A strong case can be made for Graham as the greatest quarterback ever. He led the Cleveland Browns to a championship game in each of his 10 seasons while winning four titles in the All-America Football Conference and three in the NFL. He was a superb passer and the dominant player on one of pro football's most dominant teams ever. The Browns never had a losing record until their first season without Graham.

3. JOHN UNITAS

He led the victory over the New York Giants in the 1958 NFL championship game, generally regarded as the takeoff point for pro football's popularity in America. That was barely the start of a career that included the 1959 NFL title, a Super Bowl victory and an amazing streak of 47 straight games with at least one touchdown pass. He was accurate passing, short or long, and nobody hung tougher in the pocket.

4. SAMMY BAUGH

He brought the NFL into the passing era the way Babe Ruth brought baseball out of the dead ball era. In 1945, Baugh completed 70.33 percent of his passes, a record that stood for 37 years. As a rookie in 1937, he led the Redskins to an NFL title. He'll never live down the 73-0 loss to the Bears in the 1940 title game, but he got even by leading a shocking upset of the Bears in the title game two years later.

5. JOHN ELWAY

He was the all-time comeback king and first quarterback to start five Super Bowls. He lost his first three Super Bowls, though with teams pretty ordinary except for Elway. Given a powerful cast, he took the Broncos to back-to-back Super Bowl wins. His 162 wins, playoffs included, are the most ever for a quarterback. That's not a bad record for an athlete who for a long time was knocked for not being able to win the big one.

6. TERRY BRADSHAW

Yes, he was surrounded by a lineup for the ages, but he went 14-5 in postseason games and threw key touchdown passes in each of four Super Bowl victories. He threw four touchdown passes against the Cowboys in Super Bowl XIII. He beat them three years earlier with a 64-yard touchdown pass to Lynn Swann. Bradshaw was an aggressive downfield passer and the Steeler dynasty wouldn't have been the same without him.

7. DAN MARINO

Is this ranking too high for a quarterback who never won a championship? Not after he threw for 61,367 yards and 420 touchdowns. He'd come on the field two hours before kickoff, wearing knee braces and barely able to walk. By kickoff, he'd be throwing darts. Marino's 5,084-yard, 48-touchdown season of 1984 was the best for any passer ever. He won 155 games, playoffs included, and led the Dolphins to a Super Bowl.

8. ROGER STAUBACH

He was a tremendous competitor and leader and one of the best comeback quarterbacks. He could frustrate defenses with his passing or running and turned the Cowboys from "next year's champions" into two-time Super Bowl champions. His accomplishments are all the more remarkable considering that after his discharge from the Navy, he was a 27-year-old rookie and did not start in Dallas until he turned 29.

9. BART STARR

He was the MVP of the first two Super Bowls, but let's not forget his three previous NFL championships under Vince Lombardi. Nor Starr's all-or-nothing sneak in the Ice Bowl that put the Packers in Super Bowl II. He completed 57.9 percent of his passes in six championship games and ran Lombardi's offense flawlessly. Starr showed a superior knack for calling audibles and converting third downs.

10. SID LUCKMAN

He helped Baugh usher in the modern passing game, though Luckman actually was the first famous T-formation quarterback. He led the Bears to four NFL championships, starting with a 73-0 pounding of Baugh's Redskins in 1940. Because Baugh and Luckman played in the 1930s and 1940s, giving them their rightful due is educated guesswork. Each claimed the other was better, so whom do we believe?

11. BRETT FAVRE

He's the NFL's first three-time MVP and his talent, creativity and big arm would make any team a playoff contender. The Packers were 4-12 a year before Favre arrived, then made the playoffs in nine of the next 12 years. A tough and aggressive leader, he took them to a Super Bowl victory and two straight NFC titles. He's a certain first-ballot Hall of Famer, even though his recklessness has driven some of his coaches crazy.

12. FRAN TARKENTON

He led some poor teams to respectability and three strong teams to Super Bowls. When he retired, he was the career leader in every major passing category and was the role model for the successful scrambler. Tarkenton actually ran for more yards in his career than six modern-era Hall of Fame running backs. He was one of the most productive, exciting and durable quarterbacks ever.

13. BOBBY LAYNE

He was the best quarterback of the 1950s, except for Graham, and father of the two-minute drill. Layne started for three NFL championship teams in Detroit, though he missed the Lions' title-game victory in 1957 because of injury. He was adept at dissecting defenses and leading an offense, sometimes by example and sometimes by ripping into teammates. He was not a pretty passer and was interception-prone, but more often than not he got the job done.

14. STEVE YOUNG

He retired as the NFL's highest-rated passer ever, won two league MVP titles and set a Super Bowl record of six touchdown passes in a game. One of the most athletic quarterbacks ever, Young was a dangerous runner, and his 43 rushing touchdowns are an NFL record for quarterbacks. He carried the additional burden of playing in Montana's shadow, which he could not completely escape until he finally won a Super Bowl.

15. TROY AIKMAN

His profile is similar to Starr's. He was a smart, highly disciplined quarterback who took full advantage of the talent around him and did not compile record-breaking statistics. He was a key to his franchise's rebirth and the best passer in Cowboys history. His 11-4 postseason record includes three Super Bowl victories. Aikman's efficiency may have obscured his toughness, but he'd absorb any punishment to get the job done.

16. DAN FOUTS

He led Air Coryell, one of the NFL's most entertaining offenses ever, and threw for more than 4,000 yards in each of three consecutive seasons. He was a smart and tough leader who broke many a heart in a game's closing minutes. He was the premier quarterback of the early 1980s but couldn't take the Chargers beyond the AFC championship game.

17. JOE NAMATH

Sure, his career went downhill soon after his historic Super Bowl victory. He topped 20 touchdown passes in a season only once and finished with 47 more interceptions than touchdown passes. But Namath was a marvelous athlete until his knees gave out. No player was more instrumental in the survival of the American Football League and merger with the NFL. The game's history can't be written without him.

18. NORM VAN BROCKLIN

He crammed a lot of accomplishments into 12 seasons. In 1951, he passed for 554 yards to set the NFL single-game record, then came off the bench to win the NFL championship game against the Browns. He helped the Rams reach three other championship games and led the 1960 Philadelphia Eagles to an NFL title by beating Vince Lombardi's Packers. Van Brocklin shared league MVP honors in 1960.

19. SONNY JURGENSEN

He was the best pure passer of the 1960s, when he became the first passer ever to lead the NFL in yardage five times. Marino became the second. Jurgensen played for only eight teams with winning records in 18 seasons, however, and did not lead a team to a championship. But he was the Redskins' starter in their Super Bowl season of 1972 before he suffered a broken leg and was Van Brocklin's backup in 1960.

20. JIM KELLY

He raised the Bills' franchise from the dead and is the only quarterback to lead a team to four straight Super Bowls, even if those were not his finest moments. Kelly overwhelmed defenses with the no-huddle offense and passed for 3,000 yards in a season eight times. He had a 20-10 record against Montana, Elway and Marino, including 5-0 in the playoffs. He had a 110-67 record, playoffs included.

21. Y.A. TITTLE

He made his biggest mark in the twilight of his career, helping the New York Giants reach three straight championship games. He guided a high-powered passing attack in San Francisco during the 1950s, but defensive shortcomings prevented the 49ers from winning a division title. Tittle had a dominating defense in New York, though, and threw 69 touchdown passes over 1962 and 1963. He missed his best chance to win a title when he was injured in the 1963 title game and could barely move in the second half.

22. BOB GRIESE

He operated a ball control offense early in his career, when the Dolphins went to three straight Super Bowls. He cranked up his arm late in his career, when his supporting cast had diminished. He led the Dolphins to seven playoff berths during the 1970s and two Super Bowl victories. He was a thinking man's quarterback and the ultimate team player. He didn't care about his passing yardage as long as the Dolphins won.

23. LEN DAWSON

He and the Dallas Texans were headed nowhere until coach Hank Stram rescued him from the Browns' bench. Dawson led the Texans to the 1962 AFL title and added two more titles when the franchise moved to Kansas City. He led the Chiefs to the inaugural Super Bowl against the Packers and three years later was MVP of a Super Bowl win over the Vikings. He was a league accuracy leader eight times, a pro record.

24. KEN STABLER

The Raiders couldn't win the big one until Stabler led them to a 32-14 win over the Vikings in the January 1977 Super Bowl. He was one of the most exciting comeback quarterbacks ever and threw an improbable, desperate touchdown pass to beat the Dolphins in the 1974 playoffs. He was league MVP that year. Against the New Orleans Saints in 1979, he rallied the Raiders to win from a 35-14 deficit.

25. WARREN MOON

He retired with more NFL passing yards than any quarterbacks except Marino and Elway and is the only professional passer to top 70,000 yards. He never was able to lead an NFL team deep into the playoffs, however. His long-term success was extremely influential in debunking negative myths about black quarterbacks. NFL scouts at first dismissed Moon as a scrambler and prompted him to start his pro career in Canada.

JOE MONTANA

SAN FRANCISCO 49ERS, KANSAS CITY CHIEFS
YEARS: 1979-1994
HEIGHT: 6' 2" WEIGHT: 200
NUMBERS: 16, 19
NICKNAME: JOE COOL
HALL OF FAME: 2000
BORN: JUNE 11, 1956

When Joe Montana was inducted into the Pro Football Hall of Fame, fellow inductee Howie Long did not compare him to other great quarterbacks. Long compared him to a movie character, "El Cid."

"He had that Charlton Heston thing," recalled Long, a former Raider. "You could march him out on a horse dead and the enemy would retreat."

He also had four Super Bowl rings when he retired and only the Steelers' Terry Bradshaw owns as many. That's the only number anybody really needs to know about Montana. Not that his other numbers are shabby: 3,409 completions in

5,391 attempts for 40,551 yards and 273 touchdowns.

Yet Montana wasn't the most prolific passer ever. That was Dan Marino. He wasn't the all-time passing efficiency leader. Teammate Steve Young surpassed him. He wasn't even the all-time comeback king. That was John Elway.

But former 49ers owner Eddie DeBartolo got no argument when he introduced Montana at his Hall of Fame induction and said: "Joe Montana, simply stated, was the greatest quarterback to ever play the game, and I don't think we'll ever see the likes of him again."

Joe Montana went to Kansas City in 1993 with hopes of winning one more Super Bowl. He twice led the Chiefs to the playoffs and his performance here, in a 19-9 victory over the Oakland Raiders, helped the Chiefs clinch a playoff spot in 1994.

Montana was just six years into his career when, after a Super Bowl victory over the Miami Dolphins, 49ers coach Bill Walsh claimed: "Joe Montana is the greatest quarterback today, maybe the greatest quarterback of all time."

Former Raiders coach and TV analyst John Madden, more impartial than Walsh or DeBartolo, put it like this: "We say, 'He's the greatest quarterback I ever saw,' or 'He's the greatest quarterback this and that.' I say with no disclaimers, 'This guy is the greatest who ever played.' "

Montana in his Super Bowl wins completed 83 of 122 passes for 1,142 yards and 11 touchdowns and no interceptions. His passer rating was 127.8. Yet his winning drive against the Cincinnati Bengals in January 1989 is better remembered than those statistics.

The Bengals seemed poised to break Montana's Super Bowl spell when they had a 16-13 lead with 3:20 left and made the 49ers start at their 8-yard line.

"Some of the guys seemed more than normally tense, especially Harris Barton, a great offensive tackle who has a tendency to get nervous," Montana recalled in a biography written with Dick Schaap. "As usual, I was just focusing on the situation, how far we had to go, how much time we had left, and just then I spotted John Candy, the late actor, sitting in the stands. He just happened to be in my line of vision. 'Look,' I said in the huddle. 'Isn't that John Candy?'

"It wasn't exactly what my teammates expected to hear with three minutes left in the Super Bowl. Everybody kind of smiled, and even Harris relaxed, and then we could all concentrate on the job we had to do."

The drive nearly stalled twice. Montana hyperventilated and nearly passed out in the Miami heat. He also had to overcome a second-and-20 situation at the Cincinnati 45. Montana found Rice in the midst of three defenders and Rice ran to the 18. A pass to halfback Roger Craig reached the 10. With both running backs lined up wrong and Craig, the primary receiver, unable to get open, Montana hit John Taylor in full stride in the end zone with 34 seconds left. Montana completed eight of nine passes on that drive.

He provided no such drama in the Super Bowl a year later as he went 22 of 29 for 297 yards and five touchdowns in a 55-10 romp over the Denver Broncos. Montana picked up his fourth Super Bowl ring and third Super Bowl MVP trophy.

Walsh's West Coast offense, which stretched defenses horizontally, was a perfect fit for Montana's scrambling under control and accuracy with short and intermediate throws. Before Walsh strengthened his offense with such stars as Rice, Taylor and Craig, Montana led the 49ers to the top in 1981 with a modest supporting cast.

No 49ers back that year rushed for as much as 550 yards and Dwight Clark was the lone top-flight receiver. Yet Montana and a vastly improved defense led the 49ers

San Francisco fans saw this celebration hundreds of times during Joe Montana's 14 years with the 49ers. Here he reacts to one of two touchdown passes he threw against the Washington Redskins in a 28-10 victory during the 1990 playoffs.

Otto Greule Jr./Getty Images

to the NFC championship game against the Dallas Cowboys.

The 49ers trailed 27-21 late in the fourth quarter at Candlestick Park when they took over at their 11. Montana took them to the Dallas 6 in the final minute and was forced to scramble. He tossed a high, floating pass that Clark leaped to grab at the back of the end zone. This was "The Catch," the start of Montana's NFL lore, which would include 31 fourth-quarter comeback wins.

Montana had made this kind of comeback at Notre Dame. He twice came off the bench as a sophomore in 1975 to lead fourth-quarter comeback wins. He missed the 1976 season because of a shoulder separation and in 1977 led the Fighting Irish to the national championship. He led five stunning comebacks and saved the best for his last game.

Notre Dame trailed Houston 34-12 midway through the fourth quarter of the Cotton Bowl in Dallas on January 1, 1979. It was so cold and windy that Montana suffered from hypothermia and was fed bouillon during the second half. He pulled out a 35-34 victory by throwing a touchdown pass to Kris Haines on the final play.

That same day, Walsh was flying home from Houston with his Stanford team after its stunning comeback to beat Georgia in the Bluebonnet Bowl. Walsh had agreed to take over the 49ers in 1979 and heard about Montana's comeback during the

flight. He took special note because drafting a quarterback was one of his priorities.

Walsh lacked a first-round pick and could not draft any of the highest-rated quarterbacks. He needed a sleeper and guessed that doubts about Montana's size and arm strength would knock him down to the seventh round. Walsh worked out Montana shortly before the draft and was dazzled by what he saw.

"The first thing I saw in Montana were these incredibly quick feet, like Joe Namath's," Walsh recalled in the August 1995 issue of *Inside Sports*. "He resembled Namath when he dropped back, and he threw the ball fine. I didn't care if nobody was interested in him. I had enough confidence in my ability to work with quarterbacks to know what Montana could do."

The 49ers drafted Montana in the third round, two rounds after the Giants took Phil Simms, the Bengals took Jackie Thompson and the Chiefs took Steve Fuller. Of those, only Simms became a star. In the 10th round, Walsh stole Clark.

Walsh inherited Steve DeBerg at quarterback and played him while grooming Montana. As an assistant, Walsh had developed Ken Anderson at Cincinnati and Dan Fouts at San Diego. He taught Montana the same lessons, especially how to go through his progression of receivers until he found one open.

"It wasn't as if Joe was the only quarterback who could find his alternate receivers—Anderson and Fouts both were good at that—but Joe had instincts nobody else had," Walsh said. "He could go to the third receiver so much more easily. The thought process happened more quickly and he had that remarkable agility."

Though Walsh called Montana the greatest quarterback ever, he also fueled debate over whether Montana could have been great in another system.

"Who knows what would have happened to Joe had he not come to the 49ers and our system?" Walsh asked. "Knowing how other teams operate, Joe might well have been out of the NFL in a short while. He didn't have a Terry Bradshaw arm, he didn't have the college numbers and some people doubted his consistency because at Notre Dame he'd be in one game and out the next.

"Who's to say what would have happened? My guess is he might have ended up in Canada."

Montana rode the bench in 1979 and split time with DeBerg in 1980 before winning the job late that year. A season later, Montana was Super Bowl MVP after he threw for one touchdown and ran for another in a 26-21 win over the Bengals. He was back in the Super Bowl three years later against the Miami Dolphins, opposite Dan Marino, who'd enjoyed the top passing season in NFL history.

Their much-anticipated duel never materialized. Montana threw for 331 yards and three touchdowns and ran for another

while the 49ers contained Marino in a 38-16 win.

Montana came just a win shy of three other Super Bowls, most memorably in a 15-13 loss to the Giants in the 1990 NFC title game. One moment, he was headed for his fifth Super Bowl and the next moment his 49ers career was headed toward its end.

Montana remained at his peak in 1990 and threw for 3,944 yards and 26 touchdowns. He nursed a 13-12 lead over the Giants in the title game when in the fourth quarter he suffered a concussion, bruised sternum and broken finger. Montana left the game and the Giants won with a late fumble recovery and Matt Bahr's fifth field goal.

Montana suffered an elbow injury in training camp in 1991. He had made an astonishing recovery from back surgery in 1986 season, but this time he was out nearly two years. He returned in the final game of 1992, when he sparkled in a 24-6 victory over the Detroit Lions.

Steve Young was the starter, though, and an awkward farewell dance with the 49ers ended in a trade to the Kansas City Chiefs. Montana explained he wanted to keep playing because he'd lost two seasons and wanted to play in another Super Bowl.

Montana created a stir from the day he arrived at the Chiefs' training camp in Wisconsin. Fans ringed the field to watch Montana, and one youngster crawled under his car before other players ran him off. A woman in a local bar grabbed one of Montana's empty beer cans for a souvenir. A fast food restaurant served the Montana Burger.

Montana was injured much of 1993, but was voted to his eighth Pro Bowl and led fourth-quarter comeback wins in two playoff games, including a 28-20 victory at Houston for a berth in the AFC championship game. The Oilers had won 11 straight games, thanks partly to coordinator Buddy Ryan's blitzing defense. But when Montana began burning the Oilers, Ryan stopped blitzing and Montana threw for three scores.

That put Montana a win away from a fifth Super Bowl. But the Chiefs lost 30-13 at Buffalo and were trailing 20-6 when Montana suffered a concussion and left the game. Montana gave the Chiefs Super Bowl dreams in 1994 and they enjoyed a 3-0 start, highlighted by a 24-17 home victory over the 49ers. There was more Montana Magic when his five-yard touchdown pass to Willie Davis with eight seconds left in Denver climaxed a 31-28 victory in one of the most memorable Monday night games ever.

But the Chiefs finished 9-7 and went to Miami as a wild-card playoff team. Marino and Montana traded fireworks in the first half before the Dolphins pulled away for a 27-17 win. An interception killed the Chiefs' last chance to win and Montana retired the next April. He still loved to play, he explained, but was weary of the weekly preparation.

About 30,000 crammed a San Francisco plaza for Montana's retirement ceremony. Even at 38, he remained publicity-shy but this ceremony wasn't just for him. It perhaps meant even more to those who wanted to hold the door for his exit. Montana told the crowd he was shocked and overwhelmed by the turnout.

"I'm usually one to take the quiet way," he said. "I never thought this day would ever come, that I would say the word, 'retirement.' But unfortunately it is here. You dream of playing in the NFL and you dream of playing in the Super Bowl. But you think of it as a dream. It has been like living a dream for me.

"The unfortunate thing, like most dreams, whether you want them to or not, you wake up. This is time for me to call it a day in the NFL."

The January 1985 Super Bowl was billed as a duel between quarterback Joe Montana of the 49ers and Dan Marino of the Dolphins. That duel never developed as Montana threw for three touchdowns and ran for another in the 49ers' 38-16 victory.

Tony Duffy/Getty Images

23

OTTO GRAHAM

CLEVELAND BROWNS
YEARS: 1946–1955
HEIGHT: 6' 1" WEIGHT: 195
NUMBERS: 60, 14
NICKNAME: AUTOMATIC OTTO
HALL OF FAME: 1965
BORN: DECEMBER 6, 1921
DIED: DECEMBER 18, 2003

When Otto Graham retired, coach Paul Brown said: "The test of a quarterback is where his team finishes. By that standard, Otto Graham was the best of all time."

Brown had a point. Graham led the Cleveland Browns to a championship game in each of his 10 seasons. They won seven league titles, four in the All-America Football Conference and three in the NFL.

"All he did was win championships," said Hall of Fame coach Don Shula, a Browns defensive back in 1951-1952. "He was just a winner in every sense of the word."

Though the Browns dominated the AAFC with such stars as Graham and full-

back Marion Motley, NFL diehards belittled what they accomplished in an upstart league. The Browns silenced their skeptics in their NFL debut in 1950 with a 35-10 victory over the Philadelphia Eagles, the defending champions.

"We would have played them for a barrel of beer or for nothing," Graham said. "Paul Brown didn't have to lift a finger or say one word to get us ready."

The Browns finished 12-2 before beating the New York Giants 8-3 in a playoff for the division title and the Los Angeles Rams 30-28 in the 1950 championship game. Though Graham led the Browns to a 114-

Otto Graham and Cleveland coach Paul Brown hold the Robert French Memorial Trophy, awarded to Graham as MVP of the Browns' 35-10 victory over the Philadelphia Eagles in the 1950 opener. The win, over the defending league champions, marked an auspicious NFL debut for the Browns.

20-4 record, the 1950 title game was his signature performance.

"He was a very accurate passer and because of his athletic ability was a good scrambler," Shula recalled. "He made a couple of big plays when they beat the Rams with Otto scrambling and picking up big yardage to set up the (Alex) Groza game-winning field goal."

Despite three touchdown passes by Graham, the Rams led 28-20 early in the fourth quarter. Graham completed a 14-yard touchdown pass to Rex Bumgardner with under 10 minutes left to cut the deficit to 28-27. But the Browns couldn't get moving again until they took over at their own 32-yard line with 1:48 left.

Graham couldn't find anybody open and scrambled 14 yards before stepping out of bounds. Three straight sideline passes put the Browns at the 11 with 40 seconds left. Graham ran a sneak to spot the ball for Groza and his 16-yard kick won the game. Graham completed 22 of 38 passes for 298 yards.

The Browns lost the 1951 title game to the Rams and the 1952 and 1953 title games to the Detroit Lions. But Graham's last two seasons were climaxed by NFL championships. He passed for three touchdowns and ran for three more in the 1954 title game, a 56-10 win over the Lions. Graham then retired.

Brown ran into a quarterback crisis during training camp in 1955, however, and convinced Graham to return. The Browns went 10-2-1 and Graham threw for two touchdowns and ran for two more in a 38-14 win over the Rams in his last title game.

"It was tempting fate, I'll admit, but we got away with it," Graham said. The Browns' first season without him marked their first losing season ever.

Graham popularized the sideline pass, a key to the Browns' winning drive in the 1950 title game. He repeatedly hooked up with Mac Speedie and Dante Lavelli, who would run precise comeback routes and quickly get out of bounds.

Graham's most notable innovation was the face mask. No pro football player

Otto Graham's scrambles kept picking up first downs in the Cleveland Browns' 30-28 victory over the Los Angeles Rams in the 1950 NFL title game. Graham threw four touchdown passes and his 14-yard scramble sustained the winning drive. Browns lineman Abe Gibron (34) looks on.
AP/WWP

wore one before Graham's mouth was lacerated by a vicious late hit by 49ers linebacker Art Michalik on November 15, 1953 at Cleveland Stadium. Graham left the game and came back with plastic wrapped around his helmet to protect his injury.

"That was my real claim to fame," he once said. "I had this big gash on my mouth and they gave me 15 stitches, but I wanted to play."

Graham played every game for 10 years while completing 1,464 of 2,626 passes for

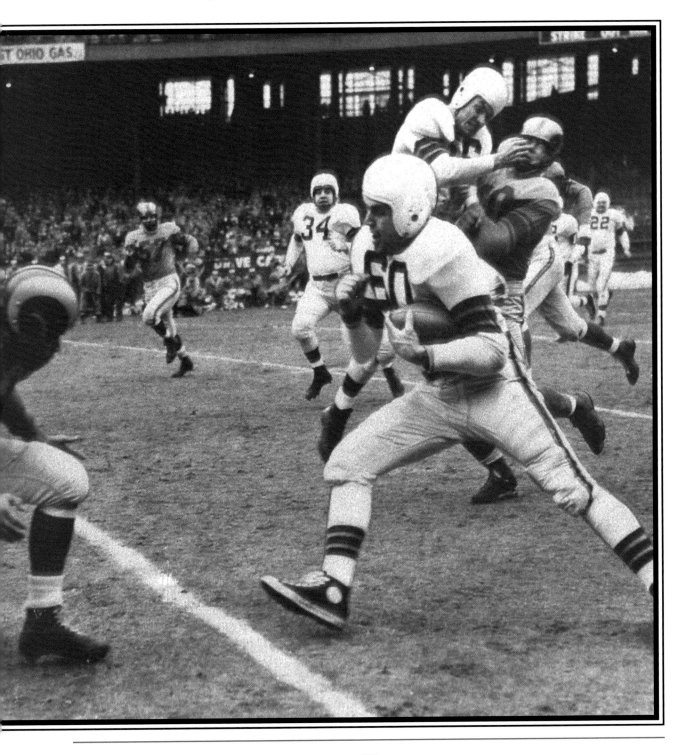

23,584 yards and 174 touchdowns. He also ran for 44 touchdowns and commanded the kind of respect from teammates you would expect for a habitual winner.

"Everybody looked up to him," Shula recalled. "I was a rookie when I broke in with the Browns and we didn't have much of a relationship. I was just in awe of a star of that magnitude. I got to know him from coaching against him. We became friends and played a lot of golf together. He was a scratch golfer, played pro basketball and he was just an all-around athlete.

Graham went to Northwestern on a basketball scholarship and as a senior was an All-America pick in football and basketball. Brown began recruiting Graham while he played football in the Navy Preflight Program, but before joining the Browns, Graham helped the Rochester Royals win the 1946 National Basketball League championship. Graham played forward and said the footwork and pivoting in basketball were the same as required of a quarterback.

That footwork was a key to Graham's transition from a single-wing tailback in college to a T-formation quarterback for the Browns. Graham's lone rough transition in pro football came when he coached the Washington Redskins from 1966-68. He finished a five-year stint at the Coast Guard Academy with an undefeated 1963 season, then went 17-22-3 in Washington before Vince Lombardi took over.

Graham returned to the Coast Guard Academy as athletic director in 1970 and retired in 1984. He was diagnosed as being in the early stages of Alzheimer's disease in 2001 and died in Sarasota, Florida two years later from a heart ailment.

Graham was picked in 1994 to the NFL's 75th anniversary team along with quarterbacks Sammy Baugh, John Unitas and Joe Montana. As much success as those other three achieved, their 18 championship games don't even double Graham's total.

"People ask me about Otto Graham, 'Could he throw stronger than other quarterbacks?'" said Hall of

Otto Graham made his farewell game a memorable one by passing for two touchdowns and running for two more in the Browns' 38-14 win over the Los Angeles Rams in the 1955 NFL title game. He scores here from the one as his linemen open a huge hole.
AP/WWP

Fame quarterback Y.A. Tittle, who played against Graham.

"I say, 'No, I know of other quarterbacks who can throw better.' They'll ask, 'Could he run better than other quarterbacks?' I'll say, 'No, I know quarterbacks who can run better.'

"But he never lost. So that puts him in a category better than everybody else."

JOHN UNITAS

BALTIMORE COLTS, SAN DIEGO CHARGERS
YEARS: 1956–1973
HEIGHT: 6' 1" WEIGHT: 195
NUMBER: 19
HALL OF FAME: 1979
BORN: MAY 7, 1933
DIED: SEPTEMBER 11, 2002

John Unitas didn't waste time or words. He was a master of the two-minute drill and a master of brevity. Former Colts center Bill Curry recalls that before the Colts would take the field, defensive captain Fred Miller would give a short speech, then ask Unitas, the offensive captain, if he'd like to add anything.

"He'd always say the same thing: 'Talk's cheap, let's go play,'" Curry recalled of the player who led the Colts to NFL titles in 1958 and 1959 and a Super Bowl title in January 1971.

Unitas would trot on the field with his shoulders slumped. His trademarks were a crew cut, black high-top shoes and a poker face.

"The son of a gun never changed expressions during the game," Curry recalled.

"One game against the Bears (in 1970), three of his first four passes were intercepted. We were down 17-0 and he jogs off the field like nothing happened. John comes to the bench and says, 'We need to find a draw play.'

"(Dick) Butkus was out there, spitting on everybody, taking the ball away from people. It was one of those nightmares and (guard) Glenn Ressler and I look at each

Baltimore's John Unitas ignores the footsteps of Minnesota Vikings end Jim Marshall as he looks for an open receiver during a 20-20 tie in 1967. Unitas passed for 3,428 yards and 20 touchdowns that season and led the Colts to an 11-1-2 finish.

other and say, 'What could John be thinking?'

"Nothing bothered him. And his last pass of the game was an 80-yard pass to John Mackey that wins the game 21-20. He comes off the field and still doesn't change expression, like, 'I'm just doing my job.' And it was contagious. We knew if we could just keep him clean, we'd have a chance to win."

Unitas' most famous comeback came in the 1958 NFL championship game at Yankee Stadium. He led the Colts to a 23-17 overtime victory against the New York Giants that made Unitas a household name and pro football America's ascending sport.

"When I think of John, I think of the two-minute drill and a clock in the back of his head," said Hall of Famer Don Shula, who coached Unitas in Baltimore from 1963–1969. "He just had this uncanny sense of how much time was left and what he could do with it."

The Colts trailed the Giants 17-14 in 1958 and took over at their own 14-yard line with 1:56 left. "I said to myself, 'Well, we've blown this ballgame,'" wide receiver Raymond Berry would recall. "The goalpost looked a million miles away."

Not after Unitas went to work in a no-huddle offense. He passed to Lenny Moore for 11 yards and to Berry for 25 to reach midfield with only 65 seconds left. Two more passes to Berry moved the ball to the 13 and Steve Myhra kicked a 20-yard field goal with seven seconds left to force sudden-death overtime.

Unitas lost the coin toss for overtime. But the Giants punted and their defenders were worn down and frustrated by their inability to pressure Unitas or cover Berry. Unitas, starting from his 20, kept the Giants off balance and had them perfectly set up for a full-back draw that turned Alan Ameche loose for 23 yards.

"If I hadn't loafed on that play, Ameche might've scored," Berry recalled. "My job was to

Defenses might frustrate John Unitas now and then but sooner or later the Baltimore Colts quarterback would burn them. Minnesota Vikings tackle Gary Larsen (77) pressures Unitas into an incompletion before he throws four touchdown passes in a 38-23 victory in 1966. Unitas' third scoring pass broke Y.A. Tittle's career record of 212.
AP/WWP

get to the safety and my excuse was that I was dragging and worn out. That play never breaks for more than two or three yards, anyway."

Berry was not too worn out, however, to carry another Unitas pass to the 8 and finish with 12 catches for 178 yards. Unitas hit Jim Mutscheller at the 1, then Ameche

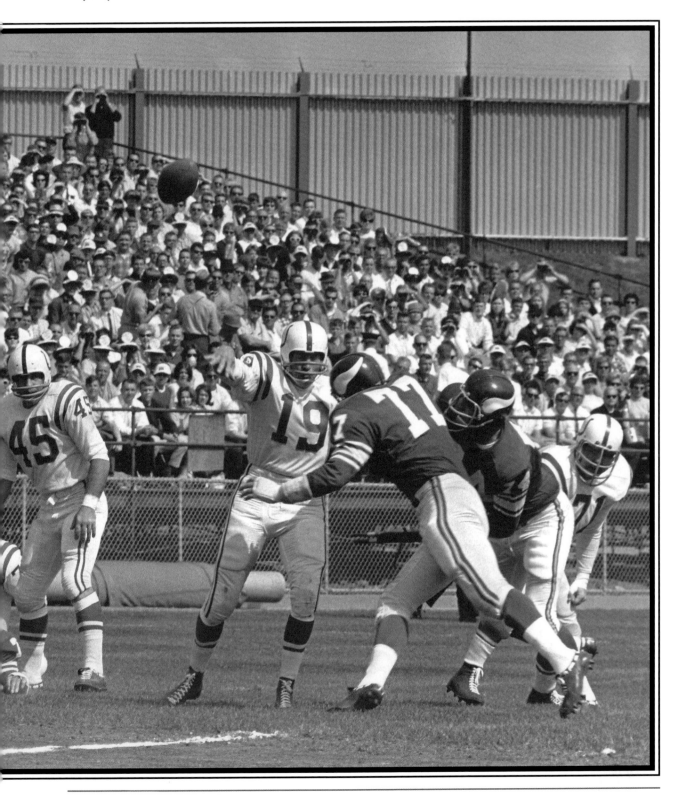

scored to finish a 13-play drive and the most famous pro football game ever played.

Reporters asked Unitas why on his final pass he would risk an interception when a short field goal could end the game.

"When you know what you are doing, you're not intercepted," he replied. "The Giants were jammed up at the line and not expecting a pass. If Jim had been covered, I'd have thrown the pass out of bounds. It's

just that I would rather win a game like this by a touchdown than a field goal."

There was little drama in the Colts' victory over the Giants in the 1959 title game, a 31-16 romp. Unitas threw for two touchdowns and ran for another while extending a streak that would reach 47 games with at least one touchdown pass. That's the NFL version of Joe DiMaggio's seemingly unmatchable 56-game hitting streak.

"He had an indescribable work

John Unitas was always a dangerous passer and never more so than when he enjoyed protection like this. With tackle Jim Parker (77) and fullback Alan Ameche (35) keeping Detroit's defense at bay, Unitas delivers a strike in the Colts' 34-14 victory in 1957.

ethic," Curry recalled. "Being a lineman, I dreaded training camp. By the end of the second practice, sometimes I would lose 14 pounds during the day. I had to stay out and snap for the place kickers and punters, then do my extra running. Then I'd go in, take my shower and get dressed.

"When I'd walk back out in the fading light, I'd hear a sound and look down on the practice field and see two people – John Unitas and Raymond Berry. They could not throw and run enough patterns. That's how you get in the Hall of Fame."

Curry also was amazed by how much Unitas, preparing for his 12th season in 1967, enjoyed himself, even in training camp. Curry, a former Green Bay Packer, was feeling the stress of earning a job on a new team and supporting his wife and new-born.

"I was walking to practice and it's about a thousand degrees and here comes Unitas, running and jumping around," Curry recalled. "I said, 'How in heck can you be happy?' He said, 'Let me tell you something Billy—you're a long time dead, you'd better enjoy every day. I love football practice. I can't wait.'

"It really set a standard for me as a new teammate. It challenged me and I went down there with a new attitude. John had a lot of attributes a lot of people know about—his technique and uncanny touch. But most important was his zest for life. He just loved being alive."

That attitude was formed by a bumpy road to the top. His father died when he was five and he helped his mother support four children as the Depression lingered. Unitas was a 145-pound high school quarterback and Louisville offered his only opportunity to play in college. Unitas was a ninth-round draft pick of the Pittsburgh Steelers in 1955 but was cut early and hitchhiked home. Steeler coach Walt Kiesling told a team executive that Unitas wasn't smart enough for a pro quarterback.

Unitas played the 1955 season for $6 a game with the Bloomfield Rams, a Pittsburgh semi-pro team. A Bloomfield fan wrote a letter recommending Unitas to Colts coach Weeb Ewbank. The coach needed a backup quarterback, invited Unitas to a tryout camp and signed him for $7,000. Ewbank often joked that Unitas wrote the letter.

Starter George Shaw was injured against the Bears in the fourth game in 1956 and Unitas took over with a 21-20 lead. His first pass was intercepted and returned for a touchdown and he also fumbled three handoffs in a 58-27 loss. But Ewbank stuck with Unitas and he became a two-time league MVP and 10-time Pro Bowl selection.

"The most important thing of all about Unitas is that he had a real hunger," Ewbank said. "This was a kid who wanted success and didn't have it so long that he wasn't about to waste it when it came."

Unitas also played despite painful injuries. He sat out two games in 1958 because of three broken ribs and a punctured lung, yet returned wearing an awkward protector and kept the Colts moving toward a title.

"Quarterbacks are being paid to play, score touchdowns and help win games," Unitas said. "They can't permit themselves to think of injuries or they'll leave their game in the locker room. Once a game starts, a good athlete will tend to forget minor hurts and sometimes even major ones and concentrate on doing his job."

Unitas missed most of the 1968 season because of an injury, however, and Earl Morrall guided the Colts to the Super Bowl, for which they were overwhelming favorites to beat the New York Jets. Morrall threw three interceptions, though, and the Jets led 16-0 in the fourth quarter. Now the Colts needed Unitas.

"John started to practice right before that game," Shula recalled. "In the third quarter, I thought about making a change. The Jets had the ball most of the third quarter and when I put John in, he led us to a touchdown. But it was too late."

Unitas started a Super Bowl two years later and this time Morrall replaced him in a 16-13 victory over the Dallas Cowboys. Unitas was knocked out of the game late in the first half after cutting into a 10-0 deficit with a 75-yard bomb to tight end John Mackey.

Mackey once said of his association with Unitas: "It's like being in the huddle with God."

Unitas' 5,186 passes, 2,830 completions, 40,239 yards and 290 touchdown passes were among 22 NFL passing records he held when he retired. He went over the 40,000-yard mark in 1973, a final and forgettable season for him in San Diego.

"He was just extremely accurate and what he did better than any other quarterback I've ever seen was to stay in the pocket and wait until the last instant to release the ball," said Shula, who also played with Unitas and coached against him.

"That gave the receivers that extra step to get open and he had the toughness and courage to take the punishment that would come with the hit. He was a great long ball thrower and his timing on the short routes, especially with Raymond Berry, was the best there was. I knew him on a lot of different levels. The best level was coaching him."

Berry spent a dozen years catching passes from Unitas and was inducted into the Hall of Fame just as Unitas was starting his final season.

"His most outstanding trait was absolute mental toughness, followed very closely by physical toughness," Berry recalled. "He had this extremely competitive spirit, linked with a great understanding for the game and he was born with the ability to throw the ball and hit the target. He was an extremely accurate passer with a full range of pitches—he had the fastball and everything under that.

"The other factor that worked so much in his favor was being under Weeb Ewbank, who gave John the responsibility of calling the plays. That allowed John to operate at his maxium."

Unitas suffered a heart attack in 1993. Another one nine years later proved fatal. He was 69.

"What made him the greatest quarterback of all time wasn't his arm or size, it was what was inside his stomach," said Giants general manager Ernie Accorsi, the Colts public relations director late in Unitas' career.

"I've always said the purest definition of leadership was watching Johnny Unitas get off the team bus."

SAMMY BAUGH

WASHINGTON REDSKINS
YEARS: 1937-1952
HEIGHT: 6' 2" WEIGHT: 180
NUMBER: 33
NICKNAME: SLINGING SAMMY
HALL OF FAME: 1963
BORN: MARCH 17, 1914

Sammy Baugh says he can't vouch for his accuracy these days, though anybody who recalls him throwing the ball certainly can.

Baugh retired more than a half century ago and recollections of his legendary 16-year career come grudgingly to him. "It was so long ago," he said in a slow, friendly drawl from his Rotan, Texas home.

Despite the procession of passers now throwing for 3,000 yards a season, Baugh remains one of the most respected quarterbacks of all time. That's an extraordinary distinction for a pre-modern era player.

Baugh, nicknamed "Slinging Sammy," popularized the possession passing game and helped bring pro football into the passing age. He won six passing titles, a record tied by San Francisco's Steve Young in 1997. Baugh won three of his passing titles as a single-wing tailback before the Redskins switched to the T-formation in 1944.

He completed 1,709 of 3,016 passes—56.7 percent accuracy—for 22,085 yards and 187 touchdowns. Twice he passed for six touchdowns in a game. Baugh's 70.33 percent completion rate in 1945 set an NFL record that survived until Ken Anderson achieved 70.55 percent accuracy for the Cincinnati Bengals in 1982.

The Redskins' Sammy Baugh twice threw six touchdown passes in a game and was a pioneer in helping establish the NFL's modern passing game. But there was nothing modern about the leather helmets in which Baugh and his contemporaries played.

Baugh also threw 203 interceptions and his mechanics would have horrified a modern quarterbacks coach. He was liable to throw underhanded, sidearm or off balance but his whip-like motion produced a quick release. During an era when the running game was king, Baugh's pass plays often confounded a defense.

He recalled to Sonny Jurgensen, another Redskins Hall of Famer, that quarterbacks of his era were expected to call the plays and conversation with the sideline was forbidden.

"He said it was more fun outguessing and out-thinking the defense than throwing touchdown passes," Jurgensen recalled.

Baugh's passing statistics were extraordinary for his era. The only expert who disputes that he revolutionized the quarterback position is Baugh himself.

"I don't think so," he said. "Most of the quarterbacks could throw, but I worked at it a lot."

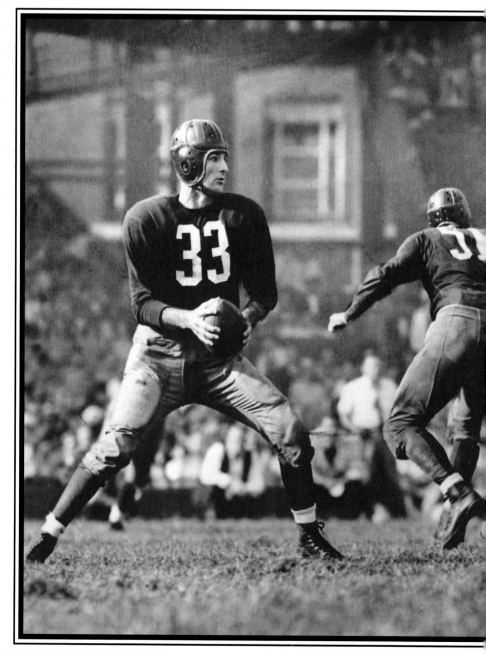

Quarterback gurus today would be appalled by Sammy Baugh's form. His footwork's all wrong and he's holding the ball too low, but his accuracy and quick release usually got the job done. The Washington Redskins were 38-14 losers in this 1942 pre-season game against the Chicago Bears but would upset them 14-6 to win the NFL title.
AP/WWP

Baugh not only put the passing game on the map, but led the Redskins to five Eastern Division titles and two NFL titles. In his rookie season, 1937, he completed three bombs in a 28-21 victory over the Chicago Bears in the championship game.

Early in his rookie season, the story goes, Redskins' head coach Ray Flaherty told Baugh that when his receiver reached a

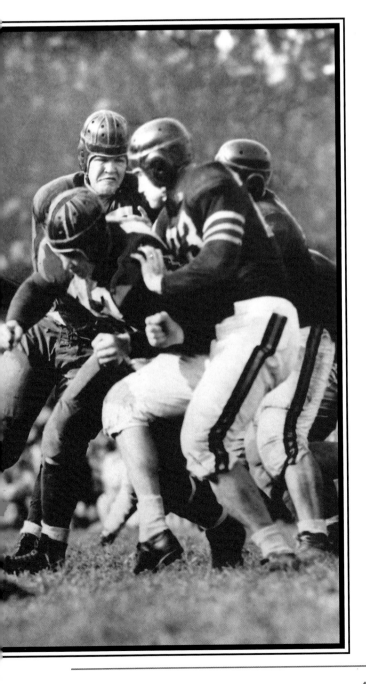

certain point, the pass should hit him in the eye. "Which eye?" Baugh supposedly replied.

"I've heard that so much, I'm starting to believe it's true," Baugh said, chuckling.

Baugh had a quick wit and star appeal that Redskins owner George Preston Marshall was eager to promote. He was the team's first-round draft choice in December 1936 and Marshall told him to arrive in Washington wearing boots and a cowboy hat. Baugh had never worn either while growing up in Texas and starring at Texas Christian, which he attended on a baseball scholarship.

Baugh made the Redskins highly profitable but that had less to do with Marshall's image making than Baugh's ability. He went 11-for-16 passing in his debut, a 13-3 victory over the New York Giants. The Redskins also beat the Giants 49-14 at the end of the season to nail down the division title.

The 1937 championship game was Baugh's first of four against the Bears, though certainly not the most famous. The Bears' 73-0 rout of the Redskins in 1940 is one of the most memorable championship games of the pre-Super Bowl era and came just three weeks after the Redskins defeated the Bears 7-3.

Marshall belittled the Bears as "a first-half team" and a "bunch of crybabies." Bears coach and owner George Halas posted those remarks in his locker room.

The most lopsided game in NFL history resulted. Baugh was asked in a postgame interview if the contest might have turned out differently had Redskins end Charley Malone been able to catch a first-quarter pass in the end zone.

"Yes, there would have been a difference," Baugh replied. "The score would have been 73-7."

He led a 14-6 championship-game victory over the Bears two years later and that score was surprising, too. The Bears were heavy favorites after compiling an 11-0 record and outscoring opponents 376-84. They were gunning for their third straight NFL title and, according to Rich Tandler's *The Redskins From A to Z*, anybody betting on the Redskins could get odds of 8 to 1 or 20 points.

With the Redskins behind 6-0, Baugh faked a pass and punted 61 yards. The Bears countered with a promising drive until Wilbur Moore intercepted a Sid Luckman pass and returned it 14 yards to the Bears 42. Baugh a few plays later threw a 39-yard touchdown pass to Moore, who beat Luckman down the middle for the go-ahead score.

Baugh's punts that game averaged 52 yards and kept the Bears in poor field position. One of their few scoring threats ended when Baugh, a ball hawk on defense, intercepted a halfback pass by Frank Maznicki from the Washington 15.

That upset had to be especially sweet for Baugh because it avenged the 73-0 loss and

gave him bragging rights over his arch-rival, Luckman. Yet, Baugh said this of their rivalry: "I thought the Bears had the best team and Luckman was the best quarterback."

Luckman did not agree. "Sammy Baugh was the best," he said several decades ago. "Nobody is ever going to equal him. Not anybody!"

Baugh was a charter member of the Hall of Fame mainly for his passing and championships. But he also was among the most versatile players in NFL history. In 1943, he led the league in passing yards with 1,754, punting with a 45.9-yard average and interceptions with 11. He returned them for 112 yards.

Against the Detroit Lions in 1943, he made four interceptions, a league record often matched but not eclipsed 60 years later. His career punting average of 45.1 yards and 1940 average of 51.4 yards remained NFL records through 2003.

Baugh still receives invitations to banquets and other affairs but doesn't like to stray far from home these days. "It's a lot of trouble to go anywhere now," he said. "I go to one or two or three of them a year. That's enough."

Baugh doesn't have to hit the banquet circuit to keep his stature in pro football lore. He'll be the toast of the old-time quarterbacks for a long time to come.

Sammy Baugh's passing, punting and defense were keys to the Washington Redskins' stunning 14-6 upset of the Chicago Bears in the 1942 NFL championship game. One of the Bears' few scoring threats ended when Baugh intercepted this halfback pass by Frank Maznicki in the end zone. Bears tackle Lee Artoe (35) watches the play.

AP/WWP

JOHN ELWAY

DENVER BRONCOS
YEARS: 1983-1998
HEIGHT: 6' 3" WEIGHT: 215
NUMBER: 7
HALL OF FAME: 2004
BORN: JUNE 28, 1960

John Elway's Hall of Fame bust probably should be displayed under a microscope, just as Elway was for 16 NFL seasons. In the end, he was everything the Denver Broncos hoped he would be. But along the way, he was subjected to immense scrutiny and skepticism over whether he would ever become a great quarterback.

He was an enormously gifted athlete who came to a city crazy about football and starved for a Super Bowl title. Denver made Elway its first citizen. For Bronco fans, he became the inspiration for their dreams, the scapegoat for their disappointments and finally the hero of their happiest hours.

Elway ended his career with back-to-back Super Bowl wins and became the first Super Bowl MVP to immediately retire. He threw for 336 yards and one touchdown and ran for another in a 34-19 victory over the Atlanta Falcons in January 1999.

"You have to put John up there with Halley's Comet—something that comes along once in a lifetime," said Broncos tight end Shannon Sharpe.

Coach Dan Reeves was thinking that in 1983 when he pushed for the deal that made Elway a Bronco. The Baltimore Colts took Elway with the first pick of the draft, even after he threatened to remain in the New York Yankees chain rather than play for a franchise that owner Robert Irsay was mismanaging.

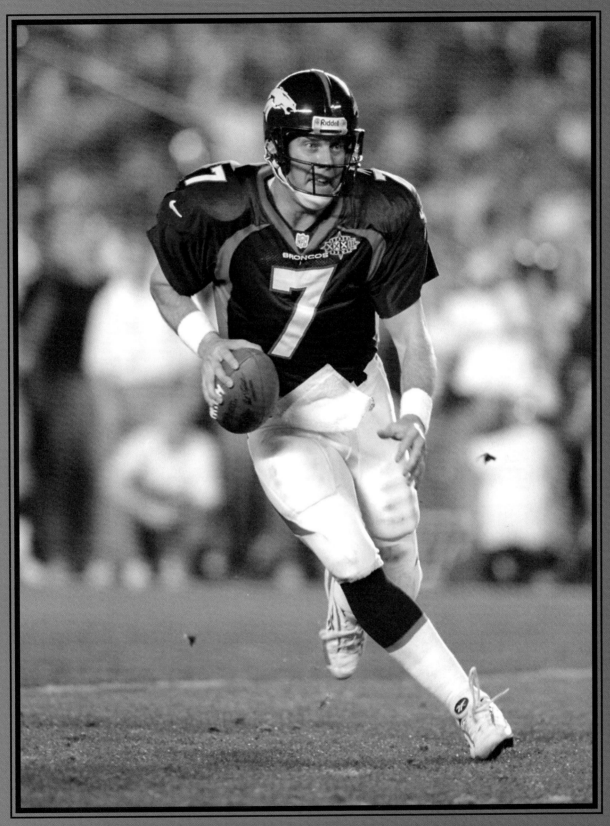

Even near the end of his career, there was still plenty of life in John Elway's legs. He scrambles here against the Green Bay Packers in the Denver Broncos' 31-24 Super Bowl victory in January 1998.

Elway was bluffing about dumping football, especially after how his career at Stanford ended. Arch-rival California snatched a victory with a wacky, illegal and multi-lateral kickoff return for a touchdown on the final play. The return ended with a Stanford trombone player getting leveled as the band lined up in the end zone.

The Broncos, in the most famous NFL trade ever, acquired Elway for guard Chris Hinton, a first-round pick in 1984, backup quarterback Mark Herrmann, and $1 million in guaranteed cash from two preseason games in Denver.

Broncos owner Edgar Kaiser Jr. approved the deal after asking Reeves if

Elway could take them to a Super Bowl. Reeves replied that Elway could take the Broncos to more than one Super Bowl.

Trying to live up those expectations made Elway's career less than one long, happy ride and he complained he was "about to suffocate." Once he arrived at training camp in Greeley, Colorado, his every move, on and off the field, was chronicled by reporters working "The Elway Watch."

Reeves started Elway in the 1983 opener, a 14-10 win at Pittsburgh. But he completed just one of eight passes for 14 yards with an interception before he was replaced by Steve

John Elway is the only quarterback to start in five Super Bowl games, though he would just as soon forget his first three. Here he delivers one of his 38 passes in the Denver Broncos' 42-10 Super Bowl loss to the Washington Redskins in January 1988.
Rick Stewart/Getty Images

DeBerg. This was a different league than he'd known at Stanford.

"I wanted to click my heels together and say, 'Auntie Em, bring me home, you can have my signing bonus back. I don't want to see (gap-toothed linebacker) Jack Lambert spitting and drooling at me anymore,'" Elway said upon his Hall of Fame election. "So for me to be standing here today, thinking about that game, it's a miracle."

Elway was replaced by DeBerg after five starts in 1983. He finished with 10 starts and mediocre statistics and mopped up in a 31-7 loss in an AFC wildcard playoff game at Seattle. It was suggested in *The Sporting News* before the 1984 season that the Colts had made a smart trade.

That opinion quickly evaporated. Elway passed for 2,598 yards and 18 touchdowns in 1984 and led the Broncos to a 12-2 finish and division title. But a 24-17 home playoff loss to the Steelers began a regular ritual of criticizing Elway for postseason losses.

Not until the 1986 playoffs did he prove to his critics, and maybe himself, that he wasn't a bust after all. He got his first playoff win, 22-17 over the New England Patriots, and a week later orchestrated "The Drive." This was the birth of Elway's comeback lore.

The Broncos trailed the Cleveland Browns 20-13 in Denver and were backed up at their 2-yard line with 5:43 left. Elway's passing and scrambling moved the Broncos 98 yards and he hit Mark Jackson with a five-yard touchdown pass with 37 seconds left. In overtime, Elway quickly moved the Broncos into position for Rich Karlis' 33-yard field goal. It was the most memorable of Elway's 47 fourth-quarter comebacks, most ever for a NFL quarterback.

"The Drive was something that put me on the map," he recalled. "I think that coming in as a first pick, and everything that I went through as far as Baltimore and ending up with Denver, and then not playing really well my first year, and getting benched, and going through some tough times. ...Then, when we went to Cleveland and had The Drive, that was something that kind of put me on the map and legitimized me as a good pro football player and good pro quarterback."

But not as a championship quarterback. The Broncos were walloped in consecutive Super Bowls by the New York Giants, 39-20, and Washington Redskins, 42-10. They were trounced even worse, 55-10, by the San Francisco 49ers in January, 1990. Joe Montana threw five touchdown passes and Elway threw none, and to many that proved that while Montana could win Super Bowls, Elway could just get you there.

"This one is going to live with me for a long time," he said. "I was doing everything I could. I'm definitely disappointed by the way I played. But I walked off that field knowing there was no lack of effort or anything like that."

But some perceived a lack of greatness. Before that game, Hall of Famer Terry Bradshaw said of Elway: "Is he a great quarterback? Nope. A good one. When you choose a profession, and if you don't reach the pinnacle, you can't consider yourself a success. He's too inconsistent. He lets too many things bother him. He's got to get a little bit tougher emotionally."

Bradshaw started a row but some of his points hit home. Elway too often relied on his powerful arm at the expense of good decisions. Yet the Broncos reached three Super Bowls in four years, despite having merely solid talent surrounding Elway.

"I gave everything I had," Elway said. "Did I always do things the right way? No. Did I look stupid a lot of times? Yeah. But I also made a lot of plays because I wasn't afraid to take a risk. I was never afraid to fail, I guess."

The Broncos fell to 5-11 in 1990 and a rift between Reeves and Elway began to surface. Elway explained much later that he felt handcuffed by Reeves playing games close to the vest until he was forced to turn Elway loose near the end. But it was difficult to quibble with Reeves' results, and in 1991 the Broncos reached another AFC championship game, thanks to a comeback reminiscent of The Drive.

The Broncos trailed the Houston Oilers 24-23 with 2:07 left in a divisional playoff game, had no timeouts left and were stuck at the 2. "I remember thinking, 'Well, now we're going to see if the first one was a fluke or not,'" Elway told the *Denver Post*.

It wasn't. Elway started with a 22-yard pass to Michael Young. On fourth and six at his 28, he scrambled for a first down. Three straight incompletions put him up against the wall again. On fourth down, he threw on the run to Vance Johnson, who was wide open and turned a wobbly pass into a 44-yard gain. The Broncos kept moving until David Treadwell made a 28-yard, game-winning kick, set up by a 10-yard run by Steve Sewell.

The Broncos lost 10-7 in Buffalo, however, and wouldn't be in another AFC title game for six more years. That loss led to a tumultuous off season. Reeves fired offensive coordinator Mike Shanahan, whose friendship with Elway, Reeves later claimed, was undermining him. Elway's future in Denver was in doubt, too, when Reeves drafted quarterback Tommy Maddox in the first round. Elway and Reeves reached the end of their rope in 1992, and Reeves was fired after an 8-8 finish.

Under coach Wade Phillips and offensive coordinator Jim Fassel, Elway enjoyed the freedom, though not the success, he craved. He threw for career bests of 4,030 yards and 25 touchdowns in 1993 but the Broncos lost a wild-card playoff game. Elway threw for 3,490 yards and 16 touchdowns in 1994 but the Broncos went 7-9 and Phillips was fired. Elway desperately needed a stronger running game.

Elway got that when Shanahan returned to Denver as head coach in 1995 and drafted Terrell Davis from Georgia in the sixth round. A year later, the Broncos were AFC West champions and had home field advantage for the playoffs. Then came a shocking 30-27 loss to the Jacksonville Jaguars.

"I haven't committed hara-kiri yet, but I thought about it for a month," Elway said. "I'm not sure I'll get over it."

Just when it appeared Elway would never get his Super Bowl ring, the Broncos won the 1997 AFC championship as a wild-card team. Davis was the NFL's top back and now the hub of the Broncos attack while Elway contributed 27 touchdown passes and his typically strong leadership.

The Broncos were 12-point underdogs to the Packers in the Super Bowl, but Davis ran for 157 yards and three touchdowns in a 31-24 victory. Elway threw for just 123 yards but set up the go-ahead touchdown by leaping for a first down. He was smacked in mid-air but jumped up and pumped his fist.

"Most quarterbacks are going to hit the ground," Shanahan said. "Not John. He takes that thing down there. I knew we had won the game. That perseverance, that drive, everything he stood for, he did it on that play."

Davis was Super Bowl MVP, but Elway joyfully hoisted his first Lombardi Trophy. A year later, he was voted to his ninth Pro Bowl and was named Super Bowl MVP, closing out his career in storybook fashion.

"I think the thing I was most proud of is that I was able to hang in there long enough to win a couple of Super Bowls," he said. "It was a long dry spell before we were able to get back to a Super Bowl and finally win it. So I think that the thing I am most proud about is just hanging in there and being consistent.

"Even if my nose was bloodied, or until you said there was no way, or until I was sitting in the locker room taking my clothes off, I was still going to figure out a way to win."

Elway completed 4,123 of 7,250 passes for 51,475 yards and 300 touchdowns with 226 interceptions. He rushed for 3,407 yards and 33 touchdowns. He was the league MVP in 1987 and his 162 victories, playoffs included, are most for any NFL quarterback.

"He ultimately may be the greatest to have ever played this game, at that position," said Marty Schottenheimer, who as head coach in Cleveland and Kansas City was on the losing end of The Drive and eight other Elway comebacks. "The guy is the greatest competitor I have ever witnessed in sport."

John Elway increasingly relied on a strong running game late in his career. He hands off in a 19-3 victory over the Kansas City Chiefs at Denver as the Broncos open their 1997 season. That was the first of two straight Super Bowl-winning seasons for Elway.
Brian Bahr/Getty Images

TERRY BRADSHAW

**PITTSBURGH STEELERS
YEARS: 1970-1983
HEIGHT: 6' 3" WEIGHT: 210
NUMBER: 12
HALL OF FAME: 1989
BORN: SEPTEMBER 2, 1948**

Anybody who's watched Terry Bradshaw cutting up in the Fox studio on Sundays could get the impression he was the most carefree quarterback of all time. While leading the Pittsburgh Steelers to four Super Bowl wins in six years, however, Bradshaw was anything but carefree.

The pressure to stay on top was overbearing. Winning was a tiger that Bradshaw rode magnificently, but he knew he wasn't ever supposed to get off.

"I put a lot of pressure on myself," he recalled. "Once we started winning, it was very hard for me to enjoy because you knew you had to do more. I was the kind of person who liked to play and have fun and I felt the pressure to repeat, repeat, repeat, repeat. And we did. But it was extremely draining.

"I know when it was over, I was actually relieved because you really need to take a mind break. Once you establish a line of excellence, that's your measuring stick and anything short of that is disappointing to everybody. I loved the big games and I loved the winning but I thought, 'Where's the thrill of this? I've got to do this again?'"

With Bradshaw, the Steelers reached the playoffs 10 times and the higher the stakes, the better he performed. He threw at least one key touchdown pass in each of his four Super Bowls and totaled nine. He

Pittsburgh's Terry Bradshaw was never better than in big games. He threw at least one key touchdown pass in each of four Super Bowl victories and totaled nine. He was named MVP of the Super Bowls after the 1978 and 1979 seasons.

threw seven touchdown passes in six AFC championship games, had a 14-5 record as a post-season starter and was MVP of Super Bowl wins after the 1978 and 1979 seasons.

"In my competitive life, I've always responded well to pressure," he said. "I never allowed the event to run away with me. I relished big events. They were fun. They were defining. But I also knew if I got my emotions caught up in it, I wouldn't play well.

"I've seen so many people in all sports want something so bad that they got in their own way. You got there because you're obviously good, so why have a down time? Just be yourself. Some can do that. Some can't. If you can and allow yourself to relax, you're going to play however you're going to play.

"I really tended in big games, because of their importance, to have great concentration. I felt focused and gave myself the best chance to be as good as I could be."

Bradshaw's playoff debut, against the Oakland Raiders in Pittsburgh, should have been a tipoff that he and the Steelers would bring something special to the post-season. They trailed 7-6 in the final minute when Bradshaw rifled a pass for halfback John "Frenchy" Fuqua. He was covered by safety Jack Tatum, who appeared to spike the ball—right at fullback Franco Harris. He made a shoestring catch and ran 60 yards for a touchdown and a 13-7 victory.

Bradshaw was on the ground and never saw arguably the most famous play in NFL history. The officials had a lengthy huddle to determine if Tatum had touched the ball, because two consecutive Steeler touches would have made the catch illegal.

"I didn't know what happened," Bradshaw recalled. "I just saw a black jersey (Fuqua's) going to the post, gunned the ball and got waylaid. The next thing, I heard this incredible roar and I knew it wasn't a first-down roar. I know it's a touchdown and I'm wondering, 'Who scored and who did I complete it to?' Then you kind of go, 'That's cool. I put that bad boy in there and I'm a hero to millions.'

"Then there's that humbling part. You walk over and they tell you, 'The ball hit Frenchy and there's a question if Tatum hit it, too.' And I'm going, 'Huh? Come again on all of this?' I had no clue."

In the Steeler playbook, this was the "66 circle post." In NFL lore it's known as "the immaculate reception."

"It was a circle by the halfback, who runs a post route out of the backfield," Bradshaw recalled. "The split end runs a post but got cut off. Franco just blocks and drifts out as the safety valve and his alertness is really the key to the whole play. If he stayed and blocked, we never would've had the immaculate reception."

Then Bradshaw paused and needled, "Or if he would've blocked better."

The Steelers became a playoff team under coach Chuck Noll but the 1974 draft and Bradshaw's progress made them a dynasty. That draft included four future

Hall of Fame players: center Mike Webster, wide receivers Lynn Swann and John Stallworth and middle linebacker Jack Lambert. Bradshaw now had downfield targets to complement Harris' power running and Lambert was the final piece of the Steel Curtain defense.

"No question it was a championship defense and the offense just had to wait on me," Bradshaw said. "We also had to get better people, and that whole offense changed quite a bit over the next few years. With me, it was always going to be a downfield passing attack. Chuck Noll knew that's what I did best.

"Once we got a few pieces together and started understanding and trusting each other, good things started to happen. When you know you're good, then you have to get some breaks and calls and keep people healthy, and in our Super Bowl run we were able to do that."

That run started in January 1975 and Bradshaw threw a four-yard touchdown pass to tight end Larry Brown to clinch a 16-6 Super Bowl victory over the Minnesota Vikings. A year later he threw a 64-yard touchdown pass to Swann to give the Steelers a 21-10 lead in a 21-17 victory over the Cowboys. Defensive end Larry Cole knocked out Bradshaw as soon as he released the bomb.

"He hit me right in the temple," Bradshaw said. "I know my brother (Craig) gets a kick out of that when he sees the highlights because I tried to push up off the field and laid back down. My family does a wonderful job of keeping me in check."

Bradshaw's most memorable performance came in a 35-31 Super Bowl victory over the Cowboys in January 1979. He completed 17 of 30 passes for 318 yards and four touchdowns. His fourth, an 18-yard pass to Swann, gave the Steelers their second touchdown in 19 seconds and a 35-17 lead.

In his last Super Bowl, Bradshaw completed 14 of 21 passes for 309 yards and two touchdowns in a 31-19 win over the Los Angeles Rams. Though he was intercepted three times, Bradshaw brought the Steelers from behind twice in the second half with touchdown passes of 47 yards to Swann and 73 yards to Stallworth.

Their last two Super Bowl wins underlined that the Steelers' offense had grown from relying mainly upon Harris' running to also relying heavily upon Bradshaw's arm. He took full advantage of NFL rules changes in 1978 that opened up the passing game.

"I know your career is defined by how many championships you win, not how many yards you throw for," Bradshaw said. "I wasn't a high-percentage passer. I was a gambler. I liked to attack down the field. But I had two Hall of Fame receivers, a Hall of Fame center and a Hall of Fame fullback. You can't get to the end of your career and say it was all me. You have to have weapons and I was smart enough to realize I had great weapons. So I used them."

In a delightful and stirring Hall of Fame acceptance speech, Bradshaw thanked 15 former teammates. Referring to his Hall of Fame bust, he said, "But folks, I'm so proud of that thing, as ugly as that sucker is, I'm so proud of it. But it's not worth a...it's not worth a hill of beans if I don't have people that love me to share it with."

Bradshaw at first did not find much love in Pittsburgh. The Steelers were able to draft him after they won a coin toss with the Chicago Bears for the first pick of the 1970 draft. Great things were expected of Bradshaw but in eight starts as a rookie, he completed only 38.1 percent of his passes and led the NFL with 24 interceptions.

Bradshaw started most games, yet shared playing time in 1970 with Terry Hanratty and was replaced in the first six games of 1974 by Joe Gilliam. Boos and quarterback controversies did not sit well with Bradshaw.

"Now folks ...we didn't have a love affair when it started," he recalled in his Hall of Fame speech. "Y'all called me 'Ozark Ike' 'cause I was big and white and dumb actin'. Said I was L'il Abner. Said I couldn't spell 'cat.' Well, y'all didn't, but some fool down in Dallas did."

Bradshaw referred to Cowboys linebacker Thomas "Hollywood" Henderson, who taunted him before the January 1979 Super Bowl. By then, Bradshaw was no longer easily distracted by criticisms and putdowns.

"I think the majority of it was brought on by me," he reflected. "I think a lot had to do with my immaturity. I didn't understand the fans and didn't have to study because football came easily to me in college. I didn't understand defenses.

"My reaction to the negative stuff was not very good and I turned a lot of people against me. A lot is expected out of you when you're the first player taken and I didn't handle that well. Had I been mature enough, I would've understood the best player goes to the worst team. I had to learn how to study, had to learn football and it took a while."

The Steelers missed the playoffs in 1980 and 1981 and were knocked out of the playoffs in 1982 by the San Diego Chargers, though Bradshaw threw for 335 yards and two touchdowns. He underwent surgery in March 1983 for a torn elbow ligament and expected to recover in four months.

But he couldn't return until the 15th game, against the New York Jets. With a playoff spot on the line, Bradshaw threw two touchdown passes in a 34-7 win but reinjured his elbow and left the game after 16 minutes. His elbow never got healthy and Bradshaw retired the next summer with 3,901 attempts and 2,025 completions for 27,989 yards and 212 touchdowns.

"I came back too soon, didn't let the elbow heal properly and wound up tearing the ligament in the Jets game," he said. "Had I not played in the Jets game, we wouldn't have made the playoffs, but I

Terry Bradshaw calls signals and awaits the snap from Mike Webster in the Steelers' 34-20 victory over the Atlanta Falcons in 1981. Bradshaw had a powerful arm and preferred throwing downfield to such receiving stars as Lynn Swann and John Stallworth.

Scott Cunningham/Getty Images

would have gone home, rested and that would have been all I needed. I was used to playing with pain and didn't realize how serious that elbow was."

Once the glory years ended and Bradshaw retired, Steeler fans appreciated how he'd spoiled them. Four Super Bowl rings almost had been taken for granted until Pittsburgh began a long wait to get "one for the thumb."

"That's what happens, everybody gets accustomed to greatness," Bradshaw said. "A couple of decades later, people measure teams by how they measured us in the '70s and say that was pretty darn remarkable."

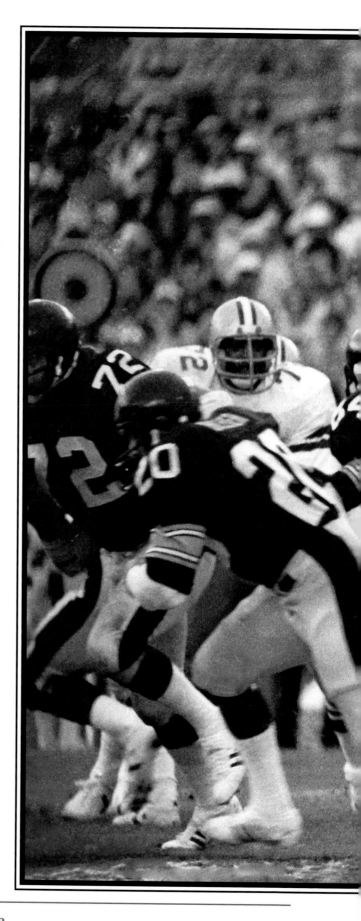

Terry Bradshaw is best remembered for throwing four touchdown passes in a 35-31 win over the Dallas Cowboys in the January 1979 Super Bowl. He also made sure that Franco Harris (32), of "immaculate reception" fame, carried some of the load, too.
AP/WWP

DAN MARINO

MIAMI DOLPHINS
YEARS: 1983-1999
HEIGHT: 6' 4" WEIGHT: 225
NUMBER: 13
BORN: SEPTEMBER 15, 1961

Even without adding a Lombardi Trophy to the Miami Dolphins' trophy case, Dan Marino became the most popular athlete ever in South Florida. Aqua and orange jerseys with his number 13 were as familiar as suntans in Dolphin country.

"Setting records early in my career and having a long career in the same community with the same team, that's the main reason I was accepted," Marino recalled.

He arrived in South Florida as an enigma, a once-hotshot college star whose stock plummeted in the 1983 NFL draft. It did not take Marino long to win games and hearts in Miami. In 1984, he passed for 5,084 yards and 48 touchdowns, the best passing season in NFL history.

"Basically, I loved throwing the football," Marino said. "There's nothing more fun than having the receiver one on one and being able to make that great throw."

Marino was in his first season as a full-time starter when he raised the NFL passing bar to an unprecedented height. Nobody had cracked the 5,000-yard mark and nobody else would throw 40 or more touchdowns until Kurt Warner in 1999.

"At first, I don't think we realized what we were doing," Marino said. "Nobody had gotten to that standard yet. We had a lot of talent and in a lot of ways it was magical. We'd watch film and figure out ways we could throw the ball, no matter what defenses would do. When you have that

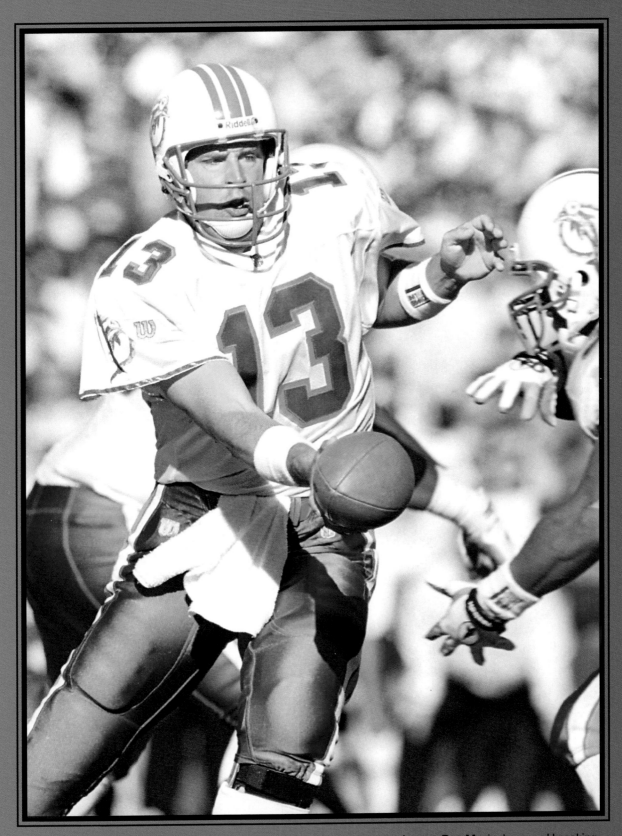

The Miami Dolphins constantly struggled to find a running game to complement Dan Marino's record-breaking passing. Marino went 13 years before he played with a 1,000-yard rusher. That was Karim Abdul-Jabbar, who takes the handoff here in 1996.

Otto Greule Jr/Getty Images

combination of talent and a coach who trusts you to make the right decisions, good things are going to happen."

Marino in 1984 led the Dolphins to a 14-2 record, was named league MVP and threw seven touchdown passes in two play-off games. He passed for 421 yards and four touchdowns in a 45-28 victory over the Pittsburgh Steelers, his hometown team, in the AFC championship game.

Marino's remarkable ride did not end until a 38-16 loss to the San Francisco 49ers in the Super Bowl. Though he threw for 318 yards and a touchdown, he was intercepted twice. That marked one of the rare times Marino was neutralized during the 1984 season.

"Defenses could not figure out what to do with him," former Dolphins coach Don Shula recalled. "They tried to rush him, but he had that quick release and ability to beat the blitz. They'd try a three-man line and cover with eight, then he had time for the receivers to get open."

Marino topped the 5,000-yard mark in a 28-21 victory over the Dallas Cowboys at Miami in the last regular-season game. Mark Clayton, one of Marino's favorite targets, needed three touchdown catches to set an NFL single-season record of 18. He achieved it by catching a 70-yard, game-winning pass in the waning minutes.

"When Dan, Dupe (Mark Duper) and I were in our prime, nobody did it better," Clayton said. "And when people came out to see us play, the three of us put on a show.

"We were truly entertainers. And after Dan has his grandkids in his arms and I'm holding mine, we can tell them that I caught more touchdowns from him than anybody else ever."

Even Shula, who wasn't entertained by much except winning, derived special enjoyment from watching Marino. "When you start talking about him, you talk about excitement," he said. "Dan made practice exciting. He had that flair. He was just fun to watch. He just loved to throw the football, throw it into tight spots. You were never out of a ballgame with Dan."

Marino led 37 fourth-quarter comeback victories, including three in the postseason. His most famous comeback came in a 28-24 victory over the New York Jets on November 27, 1994, when he threw four second-half scoring passes to Mark Ingram.

The Dolphins had trailed 24-6 and were still behind with 22 seconds left when, on first and goal, Marino signaled to teammates that he would spike the ball. Instead, he dropped back and caught the Jets by surprise with an eight-yard touchdown pass to Ingram. The "clock play" was suggested by backup Bernie Kosar during a preseason game, but Marino decided to save it for a moment that really counted.

"It didn't work much on the practice field," he recalled. "We tried it in the fourth game of the year against Minnesota (a 38-35 loss) and it didn't work especially well then. But it alerted our linemen and they saw, 'Hey, we could do that.' The Jets game was a perfect scenario and it worked."

It also provided a perfect example of the Marino grit that Shula admired so much.

"To me, Dan is the greatest competitor among the over 2,000 athletes I have coached," Shula said. "His will and determination are legendary, and I've never been around someone who wants to win as much as Dan."

Marino led the Dolphins to the playoffs a third straight year in 1985 and protected the franchise's legacy, too. The Chicago Bears stood 12-0 and were coming off back-to-back shutouts as they sought to join the 1972 Dolphins as the only unbeaten, untied teams in NFL history. With former 1972 Dolphins lending moral support from the sideline, the Dolphins scored on their first five pos-

sessions and led 31-10. Shula called that outburst "the finest half of offensive football I've ever been around."

Marino threw three touchdown passes, including two to Nat Moore, and Ron Davenport ran for two touchdowns in a 38-24 win. That marked the only loss for the eventual Super Bowl champions.

"The atmosphere was incredible that night," Marino recalled. "Coach Shula, I thought, helped with that because he had

Dan Marino delivers the ball in the Dolphins' 31-20 victory over the New York Giants in 1997. He went on to throw for 3,780 yards in his seventh of eight 3,000-yard seasons.

Tomasso Derosa/Getty Images

coached the '72 team. All week we felt we matched up well with them. Nat Moore was a veteran possession receiver and we were able to go three wide and put them in difficult situations."

The Dolphins might have faced the Bears again in the Super Bowl. But they lost at home, 31-14, to the New England Patriots in the AFC championship game.

That loss triggered a four-year tailspin for the Dolphins, and they needed every one of Marino's 623 passes to finish 8-8 in 1986. He threw for 4,746 yards, then the third highest total ever, and 44 touchdown passes, second only to his own record total.

Not bad for the sixth quarterback and 27th pick of the 1983 draft. No other draft pick in history has caused so many teams to be second guessed. Quarterbacks John Elway, Todd Blackledge, Jim Kelly, Tony Eason and Ken O'Brien were among the first 24 picks. Marino's stock dropped because of a disappointing senior season at Pittsburgh that fueled harmful personal gossip. Shula, however, remained bullish on Marino.

"We were not ever dreaming we'd have a shot at Marino," Shula recalled. "We certainly realized he didn't have a great senior year, but felt next to Elway he was the best quarterback in the draft."

Marino confirmed that opinion as soon as he hit the practice field. He took over in the sixth game of 1983 and led the Dolphins to the AFC East title. He was the first rookie quarterback ever to start in the Pro Bowl.

Shula, who won in Baltimore with John Unitas' golden arm and built a dynasty in Miami by running the ball, adjusted again to take advantage of Marino's passing. "We went from being a ball control, time of possession football team to a completely different offensive philosophy," Shula said. "We didn't care how long we had it, as long as we scored."

When Jimmy Johnson replaced Shula in 1996, he promised to rely less on Marino and likened him to a "candy store" that was hard to avoid. Johnson finally paired Marino with a 1,000-yard rusher, Karim Abdul-Jabbar, but the Dolphins still went to Marino when the going got tough. He threw more than 500 passes in both 1997 and 1998, and in 1999 led the Dolphins to the playoffs for the 10th time in his career.

Marino was remarkably durable, considering he wore braces on both knees after undergoing six knee operations and had his left knee routinely drained before games. He started 145 straight games before he suffered a torn Achilles tendon in 1993 and his quick release made him the NFL's least-sacked quarterback over his first eight seasons. He'd appear barely able to walk when warming up a few hours before game time, then would start throwing darts once kick-off arrived.

"It might've looked bad," Marino acknowledged, "but you learn over time that the game takes over and the adrenaline puts you in a position where those things don't bother you. All those things go out of your mind."

Injuries barely could keep Marino off the field until he suffered a nerve problem in his neck in 1999. That weakened his arms and legs, caused him to miss five games and led to his retirement, at age 38, in March 2000.

"There are physical limitations I would have had to deal with," Marino explained. "It kept coming back to how my legs felt going through the neck injury and not knowing whether I was going to be able to throw the football."

Marino retired while holding or sharing 27 NFL records, including 8,358 attempts, 4,967 completions, 61,361 yards and 420 touchdowns. He'd thrown for nearly 10,000 more yards than any other NFL passer.

Marino stood 155-103 as a starter, playoffs included, and John Elway was the only quarterback to win more games. The only big win to elude him was a Super Bowl.

"What I've done in my career is all there," Marino said. "But it would have meant something to me to be able to say, 'We won the Super Bowl as a team.' It's not something I think about every day. But when I'm watching the playoffs or Super Bowl, it does enter your mind."

Dan Marino watches the Dolphin defense during a 27-17 win at Oakland in 1998. He would retire a year later, holding 24 NFL regular-season records and sharing three others.
Jed Jacobsohn/Getty Images

ROGER STAUBACH

**DALLAS COWBOYS
YEARS: 1969-1979
HEIGHT: 6' 3" WEIGHT: 202
NUMBER: 12
NICKNAMES: ROGER THE DODGER, CAPTAIN COMEBACK
HALL OF FAME: 1985
BORN: FEBRUARY 5, 1942**

When the Dallas Cowboys drafted Roger Staubach, they knew the only uniform he would wear for the next five years would belong to the U.S. Navy. The nation's best college football player, consequently, was anybody's draft choice.

It was about 4 a.m. on December 3, 1963 in a Chicago hotel ballroom when Staubach was taken in the 10th round of the 1964 NFL draft. The Cowboys already had hit home runs with defensive back Mel Renfro in the second round and wide receiver Bob Hayes in the seventh. General manager Tex Schramm and player personnel director Gil Brandt drafted Staubach, Navy's junior quarterback, as a "future"

pick, who couldn't be signed for another year. And then he'd start a four-year hitch.

The NFL held its draft in December because of competition from the American Football League draft. Personnel staffs worked 20 rounds without a break and by the 10th round, Cowboys coach Tom Landry had left to prepare for a game at Philadelphia.

"Tex and I were at the table and everybody's drinking coffee and Coke to stay awake," recalled Brandt, now a contributor to NFL.com.

Staubach was an accurate passer, dangerous scrambler and inspirational leader and won the Heisman Trophy in 1963. The AFL's Kansas City Chiefs also drafted

Roger Staubach's scrambling gave him the extra dimension that made him one of the most successful quarterbacks ever but also put him in harm's way. He retired, because of repeated concussions, after the Dallas Cowboys lost this playoff game, 21-19, to the Los Angeles Rams in 1979.

Staubach but he signed with the Cowboys after the 1964 Army-Navy game. He tried his best to stay in shape, even during his year as a supply officer in Vietnam.

"To show you what kind of dedication he had," Brandt recalled, "he was in Danang and I'd get a letter: 'Please send me two cases of footballs.'"

Staubach also asked Brandt to send him Cowboy game films.

"And I wore out some footballs," he recalled from his Dallas real estate office. "But don't make it look like I was getting shot at."

When Staubach was on leave, he joined the Cowboys' training camp at Thousand Oaks, California. When he finally became a rookie in 1969, at age 27, the Cowboys had grown into a perennial contender. Staubach spent two years backing up Craig Morton, who led the Cowboys to the January 1971 Super Bowl, a

16-13 loss to the Baltimore Colts. Morton opened 1971 as the starter and Staubach couldn't afford to sit much longer.

"I would've wanted to go somewhere else if I didn't get my chance to start that third year," he said.

Staubach got his chance when the Cowboys, favorites to get back to the Super Bowl, dropped to 4-3. He took over and led the Cowboys to 10 straight wins, including a 24-3 Super Bowl victory over the Miami Dolphins. Staubach, playing in his first of four Super Bowls, was named MVP.

Roger Staubach showcases his passing (right) and scrambling (opposite page) in the Dallas Cowboys' 23-6 victory over the Minnesota Vikings in the 1977 NFC championship game. The Cowboys beat the Denver Broncos 27-10 in the Super Bowl.

"I got a chance to play in the Super Bowl before they got the chance to start booing me," he said, laughing.

Dallas quarterbacks became accustomed to booing. The franchise at first had trouble winning games, then had trouble winning big postseason games. Don Meredith became so weary of being a scapegoat for big-game losses that he retired at 31.

In the Super Bowl against the Dolphins, however, the Cowboys rushed for 252 yards and Staubach threw touchdown passes to Lance Alworth and Mike Ditka. Staubach's scrambling also kept the Dolphins off balance.

"We knew if we didn't win the Super Bowl, everybody was going to say, 'Hey, Dallas can't win that final game,'" Staubach recalled. "We knew that was going to be a critical moment in the history of that team. So probably the biggest thrill I ever had was to be in the locker room with those great players like (Bob) Lilly and Renfro and seeing Landry smile.

"I asked (fullback) Walt Garrison if he ever saw Coach Landry smiling and he said, 'No, but I've only been here six years.'"

If Landry didn't smile much, it wasn't Staubach's fault. The Cowboys made the playoffs in seven of the eight seasons he started, and he led 23 fourth-quarter comebacks, including 14 in the last two minutes.

The Cowboys trailed the San Francisco 49ers, 28-13, in the 1972 playoffs when Staubach, who spent most of the season recovering from shoulder surgery, replaced Craig Morton in the fourth quarter. The

score was 28-16 with 78 seconds to play when Staubach threw a 20-yard touchdown pass to Billy Parks. The Cowboys recovered an onside kick and three plays later Staubach threw a 10-yard touchdown pass to Ron Sellers for a 30-28 victory.

Staubach's 50-yard "Hail Mary" touchdown pass to Drew Pearson stunned the Minnesota Vikings with time running out in a 1975 playoff game, a 17-14 Dallas victory.

"You learn to be competitive, but I think that's something inside of you," Staubach said, explaining his comeback touch. "My father once mentioned to me, 'You're the only one I've seen who wanted to be at bat in the ninth inning with two out and two runners on, and who wanted to be at the free throw line (in a close game).

"I remember once I was at the free throw line, shooting a one and one, and I missed the first shot. I never forgot that and it challenged me that if I ever was in a tight situation again, I would do the very best I could and be grateful for the opportunity.

"I relished the opportunity to pull out a game. It didn't always happen that way, but if you have the confidence it can get done and transfer the confidence to your teammates, a lot of good things can happen. A good quarterback can't let anybody think it can't happen."

"He never lost a game," Brandt said. "Time just ran out on him. He was and still is a very special guy."

Time ran out on Staubach in the January 1979 Super Bowl, a 35-31 loss to the Pittsburgh Steelers. The Cowboys trailed 35-17, but in the last three minutes Staubach drilled touchdown passes to Billy Joe DuPree and Butch Johnson. The Cowboys had only 22 seconds left and couldn't recover the onside kick.

Staubach was throwing desperate bombs at the end of a 21-17 Super Bowl loss to the Steelers in January 1976 and one pass just eluded the fingertips of rookie Percy Howard. "Down the right sideline, he went up for a ball and they literally beat the heck out of him," Staubach recalled. "It was almost a 'Hail Mary.' I still think that would've been the best comeback of all."

No Staubach heroics were needed in a 27-10 Super Bowl victory over the Denver Broncos in January 1978. The Dallas defense intercepted Morton, the former Cowboy, four times. Staubach, despite facing a strong pass rush, completed 17 of 25 passes for 183 yards and a touchdown.

"People really liked Craig in Dallas and obviously if we had lost, they would've said, 'We should've kept Morton,'" Staubach said. "There was pressure from that side. We played them close at the end of the season (a 14-6 Cowboy win), and in the Super Bowl, I knew their defense would be tough. But our defense just dominated, and Craig didn't have much of a chance. After the first quarter, we played almost perfect offense. Butch Johnson ran a post and caught the ball running across the goal line and that pretty much clinched the game."

Most NFL quarterbacks still called the plays in the 1970s, though not in Dallas. Staubach contemporaries Len Dawson and Sonny Jurgensen recall him chafing under Landry's control, but Staubach downplays any friction that might have existed.

"We had a great relationship," he said. "He respected my ability to win and my competitiveness. He allowed me to run, though he didn't think (a lot of) running quarterbacks. I did have some freedom. I called the plays in 1973, so it wasn't a lingering frustration. If the coach is on the same page with the quarterback, you're still going to have the right play called."

Landry was concerned Staubach's scrambling would get him hurt. Staubach didn't scare Landry nearly as much, however, as he once scared Schramm by climbing on a window ledge outside his office. Staubach grew impatient waiting for Schramm to get off the phone and asked his secretary how to get out on the ledge.

"He had his feet up on his credenza and he was looking out the window on the 14th floor," Staubach recalled. "There was lattice work all the way to his office except on that one side of the building. I walked around to that corner and kind of leaped in front of the window. I just scared the living heck out of him. He actually looked like his eyes rolled back in his head. He was on a conference call and said, 'You wouldn't believe what just happened. My quarterback just flashed before my eyes.'"

Schramm didn't lose Staubach until concussions forced him to retire after the 1979 season. Staubach still had unfinished business because the Cowboys lost to the Los Angeles Rams, 21-19, in the playoffs. For him, that was a frustrating finish to a season compromised by injuries to key players and defensive end Ed Jones' fling with boxing.

"I really wanted to come back, but I'd also had two concussions," Staubach said. "It just bothered me that if the concussions continued, people would be second guessing—'Hey, he's got another concussion.' I didn't want somebody to tell me to retire. Tex definitely wanted me to play another two years and offered me a contract. I wish I could've played a couple more seasons. But it was time."

Staubach completed 1,685 of 2,958 passes for 22,700 yards and 153 touchdowns. He led the NFL in passing four times and his 83.4 career rating was then the highest ever. He also ran 410 times for 2,264 yards and 20 touchdowns and made six Pro Bowls.

Staubach, appropriately, ended his final regular-season game by throwing two touchdown passes in the last 140 seconds for a 35-34 victory over the Washington Redskins. He threw a seven-yard scoring pass to Tony Hill with 39 seconds left.

"You could never defeat Roger mentally or physically," Landry said in 1983. "He was like that in a game, in practice or in the business world."

BART STARR

GREEN BAY PACKERS
YEARS: 1956-1971
HEIGHT: 6' 1" WEIGHT: 200
NUMBER: 15
HALL OF FAME: 1977
BORN: JANUARY 9, 1934

It seemed like one of the boldest gambles in pro football history, yet a quarterback sneak in the waning seconds of the "Ice Bowl" made perfectly good sense to Bart Starr.

Though Starr and the Packers won five NFL championship games and the first two Super Bowls, none of those is better remembered than the 1967 NFL title game. The Packers met the Cowboys on December 31 at Green Bay with the temperature at kickoff 13 below zero and the wind chill minus 46.

The Cowboys led 17-14 when the Packers took over at their 32-yard line with 4:50 left. Despite icy footing, Starr moved the Packers to third and goal at the Dallas 1 and called his last timeout with 16 seconds left. Starr conferred with coach Vince Lombardi and suggested a sneak between center Ken Bowman and right guard Jerry Kramer. If it failed, there wouldn't be time for a field goal attempt.

"Our lead play on short yardage going into the game was a wedge play," Starr explained from his Birmingham, Alabama office. "We already tried it twice in the game and knew it would work. Our linemen did an excellent job getting under the blockers. Jethro Pugh was a great tackle (but) he was a little taller coming in on his charge, so you could get underneath him.

Bart Starr takes a break during a 34-27 victory over the Dallas Cowboys in the 1966 NFL championship game. The Green Bay Packers advanced to the inaugural Super Bowl as Starr, in one the finest passing performances of his career, threw for four touchdowns.

"I took time out and asked the linemen, 'Could you get your footing for one more wedge play?' They said they could. I said, 'Coach, there's nothing wrong with the play. The backs are slipping, though, to get to the line of scrimmage. I can shuffle my feet and just lunge in.'

"All he said, which was so typical for this man, was, 'Run it! And let's get the hell out of here.' I'm going back to the huddle at this brutally cold time and I'm actually laughing."

Pugh was blocked and Starr scored for a 21-17 victory. It is one of the most famous touchdowns in NFL history.

Starr was just a 17th-round draft choice from Alabama in 1956. So how did he reach the Hall of Fame, become a two-time Super Bowl MVP and lead one of the most storied dynasties of all time?

"When I was the starting center, he threw 294 passes in a row without an interception," recalled Bill Curry, referring to a streak from 1964-65. "He had uncanny accuracy all the time.

"Then there was a fiber to Bart because he's such a nice person. Some people thought he was too nice, but he's still the only quarterback to win five world championships. He gets left out of a lot of conversations about great players because he won three when they weren't Super Bowls."

Lombardi, who took over the Packers in 1959, initially questioned if Starr was "just a little too polite and maybe just a little too self-effacing" to be his quarterback. Starr,

part of a quarterback merry-go-round his first three years, had no doubt that Lombardi's temperament was just right for him.

"I was very impressed from the first session he held with some offensive players," he said. "You had to know things were going to change because the leadership was so evident and that's what we were lacking. He was very tough but compared to my father, he was a piece of cake. My dad was a tough master sergeant. It was marvelous working with him."

Starr made it clear to Lombardi he could be more assertive than his coach might have suspected. After Lombardi chewed out Starr for throwing an interception during a practice in 1960, Starr confronted Lombardi in his office.

"The ball was tipped, it was not a clean interception," Starr recalled. "I told him not to chew me out in front of the team if he wants me to earn their respect. If he does it in the office I can take the chewing, if I have it coming. But if later he sees he made an error and he apologizes in his office, he should apologize out there as well. He never, ever chewed me out in front of the team again."

That understanding helped cement their relationship. Lombardi did not, of course, stop chewing out the team in general.

"When coach went on one of those rants, Bart was the only guy who'd stand up to Lombardi before the team," Curry recalled. "He'd say, 'I beg your pardon, coach, it's not true, here's what happened and in the future you need to keep that straight.' He always went back at him and did it in colorful ways at times. Everybody else would gag (and think), 'He's going to kill us now.'

"Vince would back down every time. It would blow your mind because you didn't expect it from this decent, nice guy. When you walked to the practice field, you certainly wanted to walk next to him."

Starr's teammates saw in 1960 they wanted to stick with Starr on Sundays, too. They took a 7-4 record into Los Angeles on the final weekend with the chance to clinch the Western Division title. Paul Hornung and Jim Taylor, lead weapons for most of the Lombardi years, combined to rush for only 66 yards. But the Packers won 35-21 as Starr completed eight of nine passes, including touchdown passes of 91 and 57 yards. Hornung also threw a 40-yard touchdown pass on a halfback option.

When the Green Bay Packers played in the first Super Bowl, they were relying less on their famous running game and more on Bart Starr's arm.

The Packers lost the 1960 NFL title game, 17-13, to the Philadelphia Eagles. They would not lose another championship game under Lombardi.

The Lombardi era entered its heyday in 1961. Starr threw three touchdown passes as the Packers won the championship with a 37-0 win over the New York Giants, whom Lombardi had served as offensive coordinator. The Packers also beat the Giants, 16-7, in the 1962 title game, thanks largely to their defense, led by linebacker Ray Nitschke.

Curry was a rookie in 1965 when Starr in their first conversation invited him to church services in Green Bay. This was not the kind of treatment a rookie usually expects from a star quarterback.

"I couldn't get in that car fast enough," Curry recalled. "It wasn't because I especially wanted to go to church, but that was the way he approached people. The first thing you noticed about him was he had almost a reverence for people. And that commands respect in an NFL locker room if you can play. You can't just be a good guy. You've got to be able to complete the pass."

That season, the Packers were back on top but had to eke out a 13-10 overtime win against the Baltimore Colts in a playoff to settle a tie for the conference title. Starr was knocked out of the game on his first play as he futilely tried to prevent linebacker Don Shinnick from scoring with a fumble recovery. Zeke Bratkowski relieved Starr in a game best known for Don Chandler's 22-yard field goal that tied the game late in regulation. Colts coach Don Shula claimed the kick was wide right and the controversy prompted the NFL to install higher uprights.

Starr was back for the 1965 title game against the Browns. The Packers' 23-12 win was dominated by Hornung and Taylor, who combined to rush for 201 yards. But Starr opened the scoring with a 47-yard touchdown pass and led a clinching 90-yard drive that ended with Hornung's 13-yard touchdown run. That win marked a last hurrah for Hornung and Taylor, who would share time with younger backs in 1966, their last seasons in Green Bay.

The Packers had to start relying more on Starr's arm in 1966 and he threw four touchdown passes in a 34-27 over the Cowboys in the NFL title game. That put the Packers in the first Super Bowl, against the Kansas City Chiefs.

Starr completed 16 of 23 passes for 250 yards and two touchdowns in a 35-10 victory. Wide receiver Boyd Dowler could not overcome a shoulder injury, and Lombardi early in the game called on Max McGee. The veteran receiver, not expecting to play, had been up all night and threw on a lineman's helmet because he couldn't find his own. He caught seven passes for 138 yards and two touchdowns. His first catch, for 37 yards, gave the Packers a 7-0 lead.

Starr saw McGee returning to the hotel early in the morning, yet he never doubted McGee's ability to perform well that day.

"He was extremely talented—'clutch' is what he was," Starr said. "He and Hornung didn't like curfews, but nobody worked harder in practice."

In the second Super Bowl Starr completed 13 of 24 passes for 202 yards and a touchdown in a 33-14 win over the Oakland Raiders. The Packers led 6-0 when on third and one Starr fooled a short-yardage defense by throwing 62 yards to Dowler.

Lombardi left the Packers after that game. Starr stayed through 1971, when he was replaced by Scott Hunter. He retired with 1,808 completions in 3,149 attempts for 24,718 yards and 152 touchdowns. Raw statistics, though, cannot measure how much the old Packers meant to Green Bay and how much Green Bay meant to them.

"A lot of that has to do with being in a small community—it made the fan support there very special, just incredible," said Starr, who coached the Packers from 1975-83. "It's very difficult to describe how grateful and honored you were to be there."

Bart Starr gets ready to throw during the first Super Bowl as wide receiver Max McGee (85) runs downfield and Kansas City defenders Chuck Hurston (85) and E.J. Holub (55) close in. Starr was MVP for throwing two touchdown passes in Green Bay's 35-10 win.

Rich Clarkson/Getty Images

SID LUCKMAN

10

CHICAGO BEARS
YEARS: 1939–1950
HEIGHT: 6' WEIGHT: 195
NUMBER: 42
HALL OF FAME: 1965
BORN: NOVEMBER 21, 1916
DIED: JULY 5, 1998

Chicago probably has enjoyed more mild winters than great quarterbacks. Though the Bears lead all NFL teams with 26 Hall of Famers, their only quarterbacks in Canton are Sid Luckman and George Blanda and they share Blanda with three other teams.

Since the Pro Bowl started in January 1951, the Bears had just four quarterbacks combine for six appearances through 2004. Their last previous Pro Bowl quarterback was Jim McMahon in January 1986 and he was the first since Bill Wade in 1964.

When you think of the Bears, you're most likely to think of linebackers, running backs, the "46" defense and the "Monsters of the Midway." Luckman was no monster but he brought the winning edge to the tough and brawny Bears of the 1940s. He led them to five NFL championship games and four titles. Along with arch-rival Sammy Baugh, Luckman pioneered pro football's passing game.

He seemed an unlikely candidate for that historic role because Luckman was a single-wing halfback at Columbia and was named to only one of the six All-America teams. But the Bears were the NFL's first T-formation team and needed a quarterback adept at ball handling, play calling and passing. Bears owner and coach George Halas scouted Luckman often enough to decide he could be that quarterback.

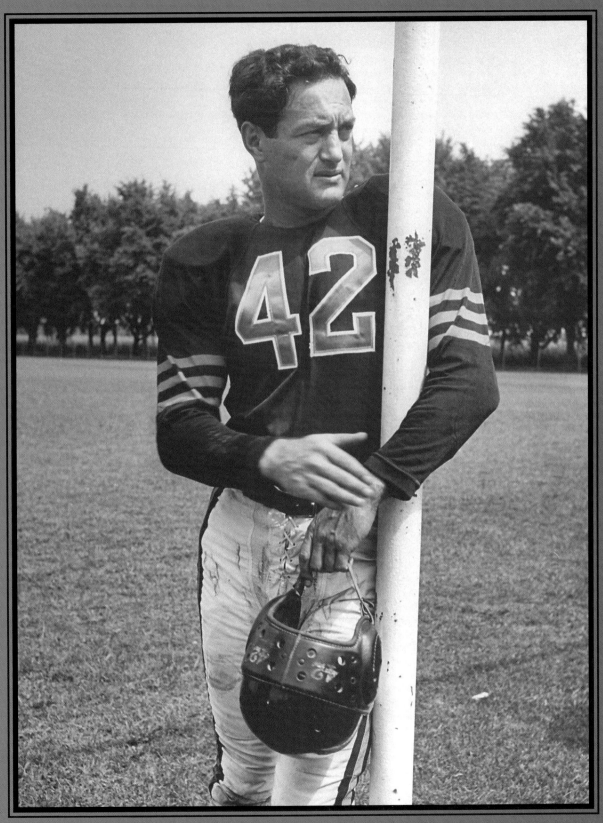

Sid Luckman, who helped make the Chicago Bears the dynasty of the 1940s, wraps his left arm around a goal post during training camp. It was the right arm that made him pro football's first great T-formation quarterback.

When Halas traded with the Pittsburgh Steelers for the first pick of the 1939 draft, it was assumed he was angling to pick Davey O'Brien, who broke all of Baugh's TCU passing records. Halas, however, instructed the Steelers to draft Luckman, who went to the Bears for end Edgar Manske.

Luckman then told Halas he had no plans to play pro football. He changed his mind because Halas repeatedly visited the Brooklyn, New York apartment of Luckman and his wife, Estelle. Luckman finally signed a contract and recalled in Richard Whittingham's *The Bears*: "Then (Halas) walked around the table and kissed Estelle on the cheek. He sat back down and lifted up a glass of wine and said, 'You and Jesus Christ are the only two people I'd ever pay that much money to.' I think it was $6,000."

Halas, as usual, was on the mark with his evaluation. When Luckman struggled as a rookie to learn his new position, Halas switched him back to halfback. Halas put Luckman back at quarterback late that season and he threw the winning touchdown pass in a 30-27 win over the Green Bay Packers.

O'Brien, with the hapless Philadelphia Eagles, had a much better rookie season than Luckman, yet Halas's confidence in his young passer was unflagging. "In all my years in football," he said, "I've never seen a player who worked as hard as Luckman. When others left the practice field, he stayed on. He practiced ball handling, piv-

oting and faking by the hour. He became great at it because he put in about four hundred percent more effort than the average athlete was willing to devote."

Luckman's work ethic began paying off for the Bears in 1940 as he led them to the first of two straight championships. The Bears in the 1940 title game faced the Redskins, who had beaten them 7-3 three weeks earlier. Halas showed his players quotes by Redskins owner George Preston Marshall claiming the Bears always "give up" in the second half. Halas also had his players tirelessly review films of the loss at Washington.

"You could almost sense that something tremendous was going to happen that day as we assembled for the trip to Washington," Luckman recalled.

An off-tackle run on the opening play told Luckman the Redskins' defense hadn't changed from the first game. He faked a handoff to one back and gave the ball to Bill Osmanski, who went over left guard and ran 68 yards for a touchdown. The Bears won 73-0, the most lopsided score in NFL history.

That was the first of four straight title games for the Bears. They defeated the New York Giants 37-9 in 1941 and the Redskins 41-21 in 1943. They stood 11-0 in 1942 before losing 14-6 to Baugh and the Redskins. Halas became a Naval officer in midseason 1942 and handed over the team to co-coaches "Hunk Anderson" and Luke Johnsos for the duration of World War II.

The 1948 Chicago Bears had an embarrassment of quarterback riches. Rookie Johnny Lujack (32) was a year away from replacing legendary Sid Luckman (42). The Bears had no room for Bobby Layne (22) and traded the future Hall of Famer after that season.

Hank/Time Life Pictures/Getty Images

Luckman got even with the Redskins in the 1943 title game by throwing five touchdown passes. Baugh threw for two touchdowns but missed most of the game after punting to Luckman, whose knee hit Baugh in the head as he tried to make the tackle.

Luckman's best passing day ever came a month earlier. He was honored with Luckman Day on November 14 in New York, where he'd been a high school and college star. Despite needing a pregame injection for a painful shoulder injury, Luckman set an NFL record with seven touchdown passes, breaking the record of six set a few weeks earlier by Baugh. Bears coaches tried

removing Luckman after his sixth scoring pass, but his teammates and fans objected and he stayed in and totaled 433 yards in a 56-7 victory over the Giants.

That game highlighted a career season for Luckman. He threw for 2,194 yards and 28 touchdowns in 1943 and averaged 10.86 yards per attempt. While Baugh was a possession thrower with an unorthodox style, Luckman was a classic downfield passer.

Sid Luckman usually wasn't much of a running threat, so when he did pull down the ball and take off, he usually found plenty of room. The Chicago Bears quarterback was near the end of his career when he ran by Tom Fears of the Los Angeles Rams.
AP/WWP

Halas returned from the Navy to coach the Bears to the 1946 title with a 24-14 win over the Giants. That game is best known for a gambling scandal involving two Giants and the Bingo-Keep-It play—a fake to half-back George McAfee, a dangerous outside runner, with Luckman running a rare keeper.

"So in the middle of the fourth quarter, with the score tied and a crucial play com-

ing up, I took a timeout and went over to talk to Coach Halas on the sideline," Luckman recalled in *The Bears*.

"I said, 'Now?' He knew the play I meant. We'd actually talked it over before the game. He nodded. 'Now.'

"So I went out and called Bingo-Keep-It. When I got the snap, I faked to McAfee and he headed off around left end with the Giants in wild pursuit. I just tucked the ball against my leg and danced around right end. I got two great blocks from Bulldog Turner and Ray Bray and went the 19 yards for a touchdown. It was one of the few times in my life I ran for a touchdown, and it's one of my greatest memories."

That was the last great moment of a career in which Luckman completed 904 of 1,744 passes for 14,686 yards and 137 touchdowns with 132 interceptions. Though he was the NFL's most accurate passer in 1947 and led the Bears to an 8-4 finish, Johnny Lujack arrived in 1948 and forced Luckman to the bench in 1949 and 1950.

Halas remained close to Luckman and hired him as an assistant in 1954 and from 1956-1970. Shortly before Halas died in October 1983, he wrote in a letter to Luckman:

"My boy, my pride in you has no bounds. You were the consummate player. Remember our word, 'Now?' Every time I said it to you, you brought me another championship. You added a luster to my life that can never tarnish."

BRETT FAVRE

ATLANTA FALCONS, GREEN BAY PACKERS
YEARS: 1991–
HEIGHT: 6' 2" WEIGHT: 225
NUMBER: 4
BORN: OCTOBER 10, 1969

Because of his uncommonly powerful arm and his common touch, Brett Favre in a 2003 Harris poll was identified as the NFL's most popular player. He was right behind Michael Jordan and Tiger Woods among the nation's most popular figures in sports.

Favre's NFL resume is highlighted by back-to-back Super Bowl appearances, three most valuable player awards and irrepressible enthusiasm. It's no surprise to see him pump his fist, throw a block or jump up from a hard lick and tap the tackler's helmet.

Favre is the small-town Mississippi kid who became the toast of the NFL's smallest city, Green Bay. He's never wanted to be known as a big-timer.

"I think that's why a lot of people like me," he said before the January 1998 Super Bowl. "They say: 'He's just like us.' That's what I want people to say: 'He's no different than us. He's just fortunate enough to play a sport and make a lot of money.' I don't want that to affect me. I treat everyone the same."

Many can relate to Favre's painful personal side. He's been through the arrests of a brother and sister and his addiction to painkillers. His father, Irvin, suffered a fatal heart attack a day before the Packers visited Oakland on a Monday night, December 22, 2003.

Brett Favre's ability to throw on the run has made him one of the NFL's most creative playmakers. He tries to make something happen here against the Denver Broncos during the January 1998 Super Bowl, which the Packers lost 31-24.

Favre stayed close to his father, who was also his high school football coach in Kiln, Mississippi. He was devastated by his father's death, yet told his teammates, in a highly emotional meeting, that he also had an obligation to stick with them.

Favre gave an inspired performance against the Raiders. He threw for 399 yards and four touchdowns in a 41-7 victory pivotal to putting the Packers in the playoffs for the ninth time in Favre's 12 seasons. He threw for 311 yards and four touchdowns in the first half and poured out his heart in a post-game interview with ABC's Lisa Guerrero.

"I knew my dad would have wanted me to play," Favre said. "I love him so much, and I love this game. It meant a great deal to me, my dad, to my family and I didn't expect this kind of performance. But I know he was watching tonight."

Favre's performance in Oakland gave him 345 touchdown passes, second most ever behind Dan Marino's 420. He also

Brett Favre reaches for the top of the mountain as he throws against the New England Patriots in the January 1997 Super Bowl. He threw long touchdown passes to Andre Rison and Antonio Freeman in the first half of the Green Bay Packers' 35-21 victory.
Brian Bahr/Getty Images

kept alive a streak that at season's end reached 208 straight starts, an NFL record for quarterbacks.

In 2003 Favre led the Packers to their fifth division title of his career and a wild-card playoff victory over the Seattle Seahawks. But a week later he threw an interception in overtime that set up the Eagles' game-winning field goal.

That was a bitter finish to the season for Favre, who once said, "I expect to win the Super Bowl every year. If I don't, it was an off year."

The Packers were on their way to a 4-12 finish in 1991 when they began to revive a moribund franchise by hiring general manager Ron Wolf. He made critical moves by hiring Mike Holmgren as head coach and trading for Favre.

Wolf sent his first-round choice in 1992 to the Atlanta Falcons. The Falcons drafted Favre in the second round in 1991 but tired of his partying. Falcons coach Jerry Glanville called Favre a "train wreck" when he couldn't get out of bed to pose for the team picture in training camp. Favre as a rookie went 0 for 5 passing with two interceptions but Wolf had been impressed by Favre's career at Southern Mississippi.

"I was with the Jets and we had Favre rated as the best player in the entire draft," Wolf said.

As a Packer in 1992, Favre finally completed his first NFL pass. It was a deflection to himself for a seven-yard loss in the second game. A week later, starter Don Majkowski suffered strained ankle ligaments in the first quarter against the Cincinnati Bengals in what would be his last start for the Packers. Favre came in and made some poor throws before leading the Packers to a 24-23 come-from-behind win. "He drives you crazy sometimes, but he's a talent," Holmgren said.

The Packers had the ideal coach to break their wild mustang of a quarterback. Big and brusque enough to command any player's attention, Holmgren became a disciple of the West Coast offense while serving as San Francisco quarterbacks coach and offensive coordinator. Favre's strong arm and ability to throw on the run made him a terrific fit for Holmgren's offense. Favre's recklessness often gave his coach fits, though, and when he threw 24 interceptions in 1993, it wasn't clear who was winning the battle.

"The way I play the game, it makes Mike pull his hair out," Favre joked.

But in 1994, Favre threw for 3,382 yards for 33 touchdowns with just 14 interceptions. The Packers were rising and reached the playoffs for the second straight year. Standout defensive end Reggie White signed as a free agent in 1993 partly because his battles against Favre told him he'd be joining a championship quarterback.

Favre won his first league MVP award in 1995 when he threw for 4,413 yards and 38 touchdowns. The Packers lost 38-27 to the Dallas Cowboys in the NFC championship game but a return to the glory days was just around the corner.

Favre threw for 3,899 yards and 39 touchdowns in 1996 as the Packers went 13-3 and outscored opponents 456-210. They outscored three post-season rivals 100-48, including a 35-21 Super Bowl win over the New England Patriots in New Orleans. Kick returner Desmond Howard was MVP but Favre, playing less than an hour's drive from Kiln, threw two pivotal touchdown bombs.

On his second play, Favre read a blitz, called an audible and found Andre Rison wide open for a 54-yard pass. With the Packers behind 14-10 early in the second quarter, Favre noted safety Lawyer Milloy's tight coverage on Antonio Freeman and led the receiver for an 81-yard catch, longest in Super Bowl history. Favre also scored on a two-yard run to give the Packers a 27-14 halftime lead.

That victory ended a 29-year Super Bowl drought in Green Bay and climaxed Favre's comeback from an addiction to painkillers that required treatment the previous May. In *Favre For the Record*, he revealed he became a heavy user of Vicodin late in the 1994 season. He became addicted to the drug, even though it caused constipation, dehydration and vomiting.

"People look at me and say, 'I'd love to be that guy,'" Favre said before entering the Menninger Clinic in Topeka, Kansas. "But if they knew what it took to be that guy, they wouldn't love to be him."

He earned a second league MVP award in 1996 but appeared out of contention for the award late in 1997. Then in five straight wins, he threw for 1,091 yards and 12 touchdowns, with just three interceptions. He totaled 3,867 yards and 35 touchdown passes and was voted co-MVP with Detroit Lions running back Barry Sanders.

"To think that I've done something that no one's ever done...if you think about the great players in this league, it's hard for me to think I'm right there with them," Favre said.

There's always been a fine line between Favre's brilliance and recklessness, and the latter resurfaced early in 1998 when he was intercepted nine times over three games.

"I think he'll never lose the fiery, competitive side of him that will occasionally allow him to take chances," Holmgren responded. "In the last few years, that's been a good thing for us. I think in the last three games, we've been too reckless. He knows that. (But) he can never lose that part of him that makes him really great."

Favre threw 23 interceptions in both 1998 and 1999, his most since 1993. His dropoff was especially noticeable in 1999, when Ray Rhodes succeeded Holmgren and Favre kept trying to force big plays. The Packers missed the playoffs for the first time in seven years and Rhodes was fired. Even Favre's celebrated enthusiasm seemed to flag.

"Football is a job and it wasn't always like that," he said before the 2000 season.

"I knew it was a business, but it's a lot of work now. I still enjoy it and wouldn't want to do anything else, but it's not like it used to be."

When former Holmgren assistant Mike Sherman took over in 2000, he made improving Favre's decision making a top priority.

"Brett tried to do everything by himself last year," Sherman said. "He tried to be one guy against the world and that doesn't work in football."

Favre led the Packers back to the play-offs with 12-4 records in 2001 and 2002. With his first touchdown pass in the 2003 playoffs, he broke Dan Marino's record of 13 straight postseason games with at least one touchdown pass.

Favre, only 34, ended 2003 among the top five passers of all time with 6,464 attempts, 3,960 completions, 45,646 yards and 346 touchdown passes. He made his eighth Pro Bowl. He's been so good for so long that Packer safety LeRoy Butler once said: "I think he should be the first player inducted into the Hall of Fame and still be able to play."

Though Brett Favre is best known for making big plays on the run, a simple handoff will often get the job done. He hands off to Ahman Green in the Green Bay Packers' 20-14 victory at San Francisco in 2002.

Jed Jacobsohn/Getty Images

FRAN TARKENTON

MINNESOTA VIKINGS, NEW YORK GIANTS
YEARS: 1961-1978
HEIGHT: 6' WEIGHT: 185
NUMBER: 10
HALL OF FAME: 1986
BORN: FEBRUARY 3, 1940

One Fran Tarkenton scramble, which ended with a touchdown pass to Minnesota wide receiver Sammy White, consumed 28 seconds. Another scramble, in 108-degree heat at the Los Angeles Coliseum, ended with Tarkenton throwing from 35 yards behind the line of scrimmage.

Scrambling was Tarkenton's signature, yet barely begins to tell his story. He led the Vikings to three Super Bowls and held every major NFL career passing record when he retired.

Starting out with an expansion franchise in 1961 could have been the kiss of death for Tarkenton. But in the first game in Vikings history, he relieved veteran George Shaw in the first quarter and passed for 250 yards and four touchdowns. He also ran for a touchdown in a 37-13 victory over the Chicago Bears.

Tarkenton made two tours with the Vikings, bringing them respectability in his first tour and three NFC titles in his second. Despite his reckless style and short stature, he did not miss a game because of injury until 1976 and did not suffer a serious injury until 1977. Defenses couldn't hurt him if they couldn't catch him.

"He runs as if he is in a basketball game," Cleveland Browns cornerback Erich Barnes said. "He takes all the skill away from the defensive back. He makes you

Fran Tarkenton warms up at Baltimore in 1961, before the third game in the history of the Minnesota Vikings. The Vikings lost to the Colts, 34-33.

cover a man for five or six seconds and that's too long. Once the pattern is over, you are fighting for your life."

The Vikings' first coach, Norm Van Brocklin, was not so complimentary of Tarkenton's scrambling. Van Brocklin had been a classic dropback passer and considered Tarkenton's scrambling detrimental to his game plans.

"He will win some games for us we shouldn't win, but he will also lose some games we should win," Van Brocklin said,

revealing the friction that frequently marked their six years together.

Their uneasy marriage was working, though, when the Vikings finished 8-5-1 in 1964 and appeared poised to contend for the Western Conference title. The Vikings

upset the Packers at Green Bay that season when Tarkenton, facing fourth and 22 in the final minute, scrambled until he found tight end Gordon Smith for a first-down completion. Fred Cox's field goal nailed down a 24-23 victory.

Just because Fran Tarkenton was dropping back to pass didn't mean he was going to throw. If he couldn't find an open receiver, he usually would pull the ball down and scramble, often with spectacular results.

Instead of making a breakthrough, the Vikings—and their quarterback-coach relationship—took a turn for the worse. They finished 7-7 in 1965 and 4-9-1 in 1966, prompting Van Brocklin to resign and Tarkenton to request a trade. He went to the New York Giants for two first- and two second-round choices. Those picks would provide Tarkenton with standout linemen Ron Yary and Ed White when he returned in 1972.

The Giants needed Tarkenton desperately because they finished 1-12-1 in 1966. And the AFL's Jets were on the rise in New York, thanks to a brilliant and charismatic young quarterback, Joe Namath.

Tarkenton threw for 3,088 yards and 29 touchdowns in 1967 as the Giants made a leap to 7-7. But they did not fare any better than that until 1970, when Tarkenton, complemented by running back Ron Johnson, led the Giants to a 9-5 finish. Given their modest talent, it was startling to see the Giants have a chance for a playoff spot until they were hammered 31-3 by the Rams in their final game.

"Without Tarkenton, I don't think we would have won any games," defensive end Fred Dryer said.

Tarkenton and Giants management had a salary spat before the 1971 season and he threw 10 more interceptions than touchdown passes as the Giants finished 4-10. He asked for a trade and listed the Vikings among his five preferred destinations.

This triggered yet another blockbuster deal between the Giants and Vikings. The Giants received three players and two-first round picks for Tarkenton, though he had produced only two winning records in his first 11 seasons.

Vikings coach Bud Grant had one of the NFL's strongest teams but was still hard pressed to replace quarterback Joe Kapp, who left after the Super Bowl season of 1969. Tarkenton gave Grant the final piece the Vikings needed to get back to the Super Bowl. Tarkenton began his return to Minnesota with a 7-7 finish, then the Vikings reached the Super Bowl in three of the next four years. They also won six straight NFC Central titles.

"He will be known as the greatest quarterback by the time he finishes," Grant predicted late in Tarkenton's career. "I don't know if anybody else will be close."

Tarkenton never was a great quarterback in a Super Bowl, however. The Vikings lost 24-7 to the Miami Dolphins in January 1974, as Tarkenton was held to 182 yards passing and no touchdowns. A year later, the Steelers did not allow Minnesota an offensive point in a 16-6 Super Bowl win. For Tarkenton, that marked a frustrating end to a season in which he threw for 2,994 yards and 25 touchdowns and was named league MVP.

"I wanted to win a championship desperately," he said after losing to the Steelers. "It's probably what I want more than anything in the world."

Tarkenton threw his only Super Bowl touchdown pass in January 1977, when he hit White for eight yards with the Vikings trailing the Oakland Raiders 19-0 in the third quarter. The Vikings lost 32-14 and Tarkenton wouldn't get close to another Super Bowl.

He suffered a broken leg, his first major injury, in 1977 and missed the last five regular-season games. Bob Lee took over as the Vikings reached the NFC championship game but lost 23-6 to the Dallas Cowboys.

Tarkenton was healthy again in 1978 and threw 345 times for 3,468 yards and 25 touchdowns. But he also threw 32 interceptions and made his final appearance in a 34-10 playoff loss to the Rams.

Tarkenton, 38, retired in the spring of 1979, though he appeared capable of playing a few more years. He finished with 3,686 completions in 6,467 attempts for 47,003 yards and 342 touchdowns. All were NFL records. Tarkenton also ran for 3,674 yards and 32 touchdowns and was named to nine Pro Bowls.

"I loved the whole time I spent in the NFL," he said. "I didn't achieve everything I wanted to, but who does? The fun is in the hunt. Now the hunt is over."

Fran Tarkenton's first go-around with the Minnesota Vikings was mostly a struggle. He calls signals here early in the 1965 season.

BOBBY LAYNE

CHICAGO BEARS, NEW YORK BULLDOGS,
DETROIT LIONS, PITTSBURGH STEELERS
YEARS: 1948-1962
HEIGHT: 6' 2" WEIGHT: 190
NUMBER: 22
HALL OF FAME: 1967
BORN: DECEMBER 19, 1926
DIED: DECEMBER 1, 1986

When the Detroit Lions needed to catch up late in a game, Bobby Layne always asked his defense for one last chance.

"We'd pass on the field and he'd say, 'Get us the ball back and we can do it,'" Hall of Fame linebacker Joe Schmidt recalled. "He always had that in the back of his mind."

Layne was the first maestro of the two-minute drill. He established that reputation in the 1953 NFL championship game. The Lions trailed the Cleveland Browns 16-10 with 4:10 left and were backed up at their 20-yard line.

"Just block a little bit, fellows, and ol' Bobby will pass you right to the champi-onship," Layne said in his thick Texas drawl as the offense huddled.

Layne completed four of six passes on that drive and ran for a first down to the Cleveland 33. Then he threw a play-action pass to backup Jim Doran, who got behind cornerback Warren Lahr for a touchdown catch and a 17-16 win. Doran actually was a defensive end playing offense because Leon Hart had been knocked out of the game.

"Bobby knew he could go (deep) to that right side because he was throwing to the sidelines and underneath all day," recalled Schmidt, a rookie in 1953. "Jim ran a good pattern and Bobby laid it out there. It was a helluva pass and a helluva catch."

Face masks were not yet invented when Bobby Layne was a Chicago Bears rookie in 1948. But the feisty Lane wouldn't wear one even when most quarterbacks were happy to start using the protection when it was introduced during the mid-1950s.

That was the Lions' second straight championship game victory over the Browns, who were in the midst of their dynasty. In a 17-7 title game win in 1952, Layne scored on a two-yard plunge and Doak Walker scored on a 67-yard run.

The Browns regained the title in 1954 by beating the Lions 56-10. Layne also led the Lions in their championship season of 1957 until he suffered a broken leg against the Browns in the next-to-last regular-season game. He spent his fourth title game watching Tobin Rote lead a 59-14 victory over the Browns.

For all his success, Layne was far from a picture passer. His fundamentals were poor and he threw 47 more interceptions than touchdown passes.

"A lot of people disregard his athletic ability, but I'd say he was a little better than average runner and his arm strength was average to good," recalled Schmidt, who later also coached the Lions.

"He did not have a great arm like Unitas, Elway and people like that. But he had an uncanny ability of being able to understand the game. He knew exactly what had to be done to take a defense apart and how to go to certain places at certain times and he'd be accurate with his passes. The ball didn't always look like a dart. Sometimes it would have a little loop to it. But it would find its way there."

San Francisco 49ers coach Red Hickey once said: "Now, Layne, as bad as he looked throwing the ball, was a winner. You'd work him out and you wouldn't want him. But you'd want him in your huddle. Players feel that way about a quarterback. When a leader is in there, they'll perform, they'll go."

Layne led his teammates with fire on the field and a good time off the field. Schmidt recalls a game in 1953 when Layne came down hard on rookie tackle Oliver Spencer because he was struggling to block his man.

"Oliver was not having a good day," Schmidt recalled. "They were beating him and Bobby actually stopped the game and went over to the sideline and told Buddy Parker, 'If you don't get him out of the game, I'm coming out.' They made some shifts on the line and Ollie came out. He almost had Ollie in tears.

"Bobby wasn't very sympathetic in regard to if you were a rookie or who you were. In fact, he'd always say, 'You want to come back here and throw this ball? If you do, I'll take your spot on the line.'"

No wonder Hall of Fame tackle Lou Creekmur once said: "We all made a pact that we would never miss a block that would ever disturb Bobby Layne."

Layne figured any hard feelings could be soothed on Mondays when he took his teammates to a bar near Briggs Stadium, the Lions' home. Schmidt recalls Layne did not look kindly upon teammates who did not join his happy hour.

"The biggest thing about our success was the tightness of the group," Layne said.

"You showed up whether you drank or not. We had 100 percent attendance. The worst thing that could happen was if a couple of players went somewhere else. Pretty soon, those two are blaming the other two for something that went wrong. We'd meet, go over Sunday's game and iron out any differences we had. We all left there as friends and if we had a loss, by Tuesday we'd have it behind us and be ready for the next game. Nobody was blamin' anyone else."

Layne did not drink just on Mondays, however. He was arrested for driving while intoxicated early in the 1957 season and, according to the *Detroit Free Press*, was acquitted after insisting the arresting officer had mistaken his slow Texas drawl for slurred speech. The Lions trainer hung a sign over Layne's locker that read: "I'm Not Drunk. I'm Just From Texas."

Layne's drinking has inspired considerable lore, without shedding much light on just how severe a problem he might have had.

"It's hard to draw a line in that respect," Schmidt said. "It all depends how you're looking at it, what kind of friend you were, what you saw happen. At times he drank to excess. Guys I played against said he was drunk on the field, which I never saw.

"Did he drink the night before the game? At times, I guess. I never saw him in a game or prior to a game out of control. He liked to have a good time and I think most of his good time was having the team together and he thought there was no better way than to have guys hang out and create camaraderie. His theory was: we're going to play together, we're going to party together, we're going to be happy or sad together.

"He did drink. I don't want to paint him as a saint, but I think it was exaggerated to a point. He would give people the idea, 'Maybe I'm not fit to play,' and then enjoy throwing those sons of guns off the field. I think he enjoyed being one up on you."

Schmidt also suggests the happy-go-lucky stereotype of Layne belied his complexities. Schmidt said he sensed some underlying unhappiness in a star who was six when his father died and he was adopted by an aunt and uncle in Fort Worth, Texas.

"Everybody thought he was just a good-time guy but there was a deepness to him a lot of people didn't know about," Schmidt said. "He was never real talkative about his past, his relationship with his family and some of the things he did maybe masked some of the unhappiness he had. He was a deep thinker. He knew about the personalities of people, what made them tick. I think he was a lot more sensitive to things than people give him credit for.

"I enjoyed him, I enjoyed playing with him. You knew he was going to give you 100 percent. You knew he wanted to win passionately and that's all you can ask of a guy. He was always prepared to play to the best of his ability and he didn't want to tolerate anybody who couldn't give him 100 percent. I respected him, I thought he was a damn good football player and a guy who loved the game and gave it everything he had."

Layne was a first-round pick of the Chicago Bears in 1948 but sat behind Sid Luckman and Johnny Lujack and was traded after one season to the lowly New York Bulldogs. Layne received a huge break when he was traded to the Lions and rejoined Walker, a high school teammate who became a Hall of Fame halfback.

Layne moved right into a starting job in 1950. A year later the Lions hired Parker, a player's coach whose easygoing style suited Layne just fine.

"Buddy was very lax as far as rules," Schmidt recalled. "He knew Layne wasn't going to keep the rules."

Layne in 1951 threw for 2,403 yards and 26 touchdowns, a club record that stood until Scott Mitchell threw 32 touchdown passes in 1995. Layne in 1952 threw for 1,999 yards and 19 touchdowns and ran for 411 yards while leading the Lions to their first of three straight championship games. He continued to play without a face-mask even when the protective bar was gaining acceptance.

Parker left for Pittsburgh in 1957 and early the next season acquired Layne for quarterback Earl Morrall and two draft picks. Lions coach George Wilson was splitting time between Layne and Rote in 1958 and Layne got off to a slow start and needed a change of scenery. He made an immediate impact for the Steelers, who stood 0-2 after a 45-12 home loss to the Browns. Layne led the Steelers to a 24-3 upset of the Eagles and a 7-4-1 record, the franchise's best since 1947.

"Layne turned us into a football team," Parker said. "He's the only guy who could have made so much difference so fast."

Layne promised he would not retire until he led the Steelers to a championship but had to settle for going out with a 9-5 record in 1962. He completed 1,814 of 3,700 passes for 26,768 yards and 196 touchdowns.

Layne died just before his 60th birthday. He always did say, "The secret to a happy life is to run out of cash and air at the same time."

Bobby Layne, left, found formidable competition when he joined the Chicago Bears in 1948. Sid Luckman, middle, was an all-time great and Johnny Lujack, right, was being groomed to succeed Luckman. Though Layne couldn't find a place in Chicago, he found one in the Pro Football Hall of Fame.

STEVE YOUNG

14

LOS ANGELES EXPRESS, TAMPA BAY BUCCANEERS,
SAN FRANCISCO 49ERS
YEARS: 1984-1999
HEIGHT: 6' 2" WEIGHT: 205
NUMBER: 8
BORN: OCTOBER 11, 1961

Steve Young would have packed up and gone home early in his professional career had he bowed to every skeptic and negative scouting report. When he came out of Brigham Young, supposedly all Young could do was run. He developed into the NFL's highest-rated passer of all time.

"My whole career," Young said, "I wanted to make a statement: 'Yes, you could be a scrambler but you could also be a really top, efficient pocket passer.'

"The scrambler always gets people's eyes, like fireworks. You tend to look up. If you're not careful, you lose appreciation for everything that's happening in the pocket. People tended to remember the touchdown runs more than they remembered the throws."

A good example was Young's final game at Brigham Young, a 21-17 victory over Missouri in the 1983 Holiday Bowl. He handed off to running back Eddie Stinnett, who faked a sweep right and threw back across the field to Young for a 14-yard touchdown play with 23 seconds left. Young had a touchdown run, pass and catch for the night, but his razzle dazzle at the end would be best remembered.

He threw for 3,902 yards and 33 touchdowns his senior year, had good size and could run like a deer. So why weren't NFL teams salivating to sign him?

Steve Young watches the 49er defense in a 28-14 victory over the Phoenix Cardinals in 1993. That was Young's first season with Joe Montana gone from San Francisco, yet Young never did escape Montana's shadow until he won a Super Bowl a season later.

Brigham Young quarterbacks were suspect because of their passer-friendly system and most, except Jim McMahon, fell short as pros. Young is a descendant of Brigham Young and was not about to play anywhere else.

He signed with the Los Angeles Express of the United States Football League in 1984 and became the first pro ever to pass for 300 yards and rush for 100 yards in one game. He briefly became a running back when injuries reduced the Express offense to 11 players and there was no cash to sign replacements. When the USFL folded in the summer of 1985, Young joined the Tampa Bay Buccaneers as Steve DeBerg's backup.

Young started in 1986 but after a 2-14 finish went to San Francisco for second- and fourth-round draft picks and cash. The Bucs owned the first pick in the 1987 draft and took Heisman Trophy winner Vinny Testaverde. That allowed them to trade a player who would win a Super Bowl, two league MVP awards and six passing titles.

San Francisco coach Bill Walsh had won two Super Bowls with Joe Montana, who was still in his prime. Walsh needed a

For all of Steve Young's record-breaking passing performances, his brilliant runs usually evoked the most oohs and aahs. He takes off in the San Francisco 49ers' 26-21 loss at Buffalo in 1998 as Bills end Marcellus Wiley (75) gives chase.
Rick Stewart/Getty Images

107

TROY AIKMAN

DALLAS COWBOYS
YEARS: 1989-2000
HEIGHT: 6' 4" WEIGHT: 216
NUMBER: 8
BORN: NOVEMBER 21, 1966

Because Troy Aikman was the top pick of the 1989 draft, some might be inclined to take his three Super Bowl wins for granted.

Though winning a Super Bowl is the popular expectation for quarterbacks drafted first overall, few live up to it. In the 15 drafts after the Cowboys picked Aikman, eight quarterbacks have been top overall picks. All were still seeking their first championship when quarterback Eli Manning became the top pick in 2004. Only one of those top picks, former New England Patriot Drew Bledsoe, has led a team to a Super Bowl.

Aikman gave new coach Jimmy Johnson a major building block for a team that grew in four years from a 1-15 doormat to a Super Bowl champion. Aikman made his postseason debut in 1992 by throwing eight touchdown passes and no interceptions in three games. He was named Super Bowl MVP after completing 22 of 30 passes for 273 yards and four touchdowns in a 52-17 victory over the Buffalo Bills.

"I still don't fully understand the scope of what we've done," Aikman said after receiving his MVP trophy. "But slowly I'm beginning to realize that I now have a place in history with some other quarterbacks. The last two seasons, even though I'd had success, I don't think people perceived me as a top-notch quarterback.

Troy Aikman shows the pinpoint accuracy that helped take the Dallas Cowboys to three Super Bowl wins. Here he attacks the Arizona Cardinals in a 48-7 Dallas victory in 2000, Aikman's final season.

"It took the Super Bowl for me to break out of that image. I know a tremendous weight has been taken off my shoulders because where I was drafted, this is what's expected. You're expected to win a Super Bowl."

Aikman has more Super Bowl victories than any other quarterbacks except San Francisco's Joe Montana and Pittsburgh's Terry Bradshaw. Each won four.

A quarterback drafted number one also is expected to amass record-breaking statistics. Aikman did not. Though he enjoyed five 3,000-yard seasons, he never threw more than 23 touchdown passes in a year and wasn't fixated on personal statistics.

"He was a terrible fantasy football quarterback," joked Gil Brandt, former Cowboys director of player personnel who bowed out with the 1989 draft. "Emmitt (Smith) was a great fantasy player and Aikman was not. But Aikman probably was as accurate as any quarterback I've ever seen. The guy was amazing. It was almost as if the ball was on a string."

Aikman, Smith and Michael Irvin were the Triplets. That passer, runner and receiver led the Dallas offense to three

Troy Aikman zips a pass over Pittsburgh Steeler defenders Chad Brown (94) and Levon Kirkland (99) in the Dallas Cowboys' 27-17 Super Bowl victory in January 1996.
Al Bello/Getty Images

Super Bowl wins in four years. The Cowboys beat the Bills again, 30-13, in January 1994. They beat the Pittsburgh Steelers, 27-17, two years later.

"All three of us stepped up," said Smith, who scored 164 touchdowns as a Cowboy. "We all pushed one another. (Aikman) probably was the laid back one, but he was the stubborn one, too. His stubbornness was really his way of showing that losing was not an option. That strong arm, the blond hair and blue eyes—his legacy is part of the Dallas Cowboys. Any time you saw us winning, you saw him throwing."

During the 1990s Aikman won 112 games, playoffs included. No other quarterback ever has won as many games in one decade.

Because of the Cowboys' reliance upon Smith, may questioned if Aikman in a pinch could carry the offense with his arm. He answered that in the 1994 NFC championship game at San Francisco. The Cowboys fell behind 21-0 in the first five minutes, and Aikman, forced to ditch his running game, completed 30 of 53 passes for 380 yards and two touchdowns to Michael Irvin. The 49ers sacked Aikman four times and gave him a pounding, but he kept fighting to rally the Cowboys in a 38-28 loss.

"When you're able to get up every morning for the last 12 years knowing you have a franchise quarterback, that's a luxury in the NFL," Cowboys owner Jerry Jones told the *Dallas Morning News* in 2001.

Jones enjoyed that luxury because Johnson made the right call on draft day. Aikman showcased his passing at UCLA once he transferred from Oklahoma, where he had been miscast as a wishbone quarterback.

Brandt recalls the Cowboys weren't sure whether to take Aikman or Tony Mandarich, a massive tackle from Michigan who became one of the biggest busts in draft history. Johnson, the former University of Miami coach, and Brandt attended Aikman's predraft workout.

"The guy had some knocks on him," Brandt recalled. "They had played Washington State (a 34-30 upset winner) and the ball was on the five-yard line with a minute to go and they couldn't score and there was some talk, 'Well, Aikman couldn't do the big-game thing.' I guess on three plays they had the wrong personnel on the field.

"The guy threw passes for an hour and never threw one bad ball. So on the way back to the airplane I said to Jimmy, 'What do you think of Aikman now?' Jimmy said, 'Well, if we had Aikman at Miami, we'd have been 24-0 instead of 23-1 (his last two years) and won every game by 50 points.'"

Johnson had the misfortune of watching Aikman from the opposite sideline in 1996 when Johnson, fired by Jones after the 1993 season, took over the Miami Dolphins. Aikman completed 33 of 41 passes for 363 yards and three touchdowns in a 29-10 victory that ended with Jones futilely urging coach Barry Switzer to run up the score.

Aikman led the Cowboys to the playoffs eight times during the 1990s and opened the 1999 season at Washington by orchestrating the biggest comeback in franchise history. The Cowboys were 21 points behind in the fourth quarter but tied the score after a second touchdown pass to Irvin with just under two minutes left. Aikman's 76-yard touchdown pass to Rocket Ismail in overtime climaxed a 41-35 victory.

Aikman enjoyed his last successful season in 1999. His 2000 season ended with a concussion in week 14 caused by a leaping tackle by Redskins linebacker LaVar Arrington. That was Aikman's second concussion of the season and 10th of his career. He twice needed epidural injections in 2000 to treat severe back pains.

Aikman missed five games because of injuries that year and was knocked out early in three other games. He was only 34 but, like Cowboys Hall of Fame quarterback Roger Staubach, saw concussions force his early retirement.

Rather than commit valuable salary cap space to a quarterback in questionable health, the Cowboys waived Aikman in March 2001. He retired in April and started a successful broadcasting career.

"He is the consummate team player," Jones said. "He never complained about throwing the ball more and getting better statistics. All he cared about was winning."

Aikman completed 2,898 of 4,715 passes for 32,942 yards and 165 touchdowns and 141 interceptions. He was a six-time Pro Bowl pick.

"I don't think you fully understand what it's like to play for a franchise like the Dallas Cowboys until you do it," Aikman said upon retiring. "The success we had just made it more special. It came with some heartache and tough times, but I have no regrets. It was a great 12 years. It was the experience of a lifetime, and I wouldn't change a thing about my time in Dallas."

Aikman retired as the Cowboys' leader in every major passing category. But he's remembered in Dallas for being much more than that.

"Put him right up there with Captain America (Staubach) and Mr. Cowboy (Bob Lilly)," said longtime Cowboy Bill Bates. "He's done as much for this organization as far as class and winning as anybody to ever wear the star."

The last two of the Dallas Cowboys' triplets, Emmitt Smith (22) and Troy Aikman, team up for one of the last times in a 23-6 victory over the Cincinnati Bengals in 2000. A history of concussions forced Aikman to retire after that season.

Jamie Squire/Getty Images

DAN FOUTS

SAN DIEGO CHARGERS
YEARS: 1973-1987
HEIGHT: 6' 3" WEIGHT: 210
NUMBER: 14
HALL OF FAME: 1993
BORN: JUNE 10, 1951

You would not have wanted to be playing defense when Air Coryell was flying high. Every San Diego runner and receiver was a threat to score every play.

The wide receivers included Charlie Joiner, John Jefferson and Wes Chandler. Kellen Winslow was the best pass-catching tight end of his era. Chuck Muncie was a threat as a runner and receiver and James Brooks was an explosive third-down back. Don Coryell's quarterback was Dan Fouts, a smart and tough leader who knew exactly how to use his wonderful weapons.

"We had the feeling of being unstoppable, which was nice," recalled Fouts, who topped 4,000 yards passing in 1979, 1980

and 1981. "It was almost as if the defense wasn't even there.

"We practiced with a game-like intensity and it really helped us. When you have talent like we did, the real credit goes to each one of those guys. They would have been superstars by themselves but they fit into the team concept and didn't let the fact they weren't getting the ball every down affect them.

"They competed to get the ball each down. All of them wanted to be the difference maker, the guy who kept the drive alive, who got the touchdown. It was a real healthy situation."

Joiner and Winslow also are in the Hall of Fame. Muncie, Chandler and Jefferson,

Dan Fouts comes out throwing at Kansas City in the 1987 opener. The Chargers lost 20-13 just before starting an eight-game winning streak.

Jonathan Daniel/Getty Images

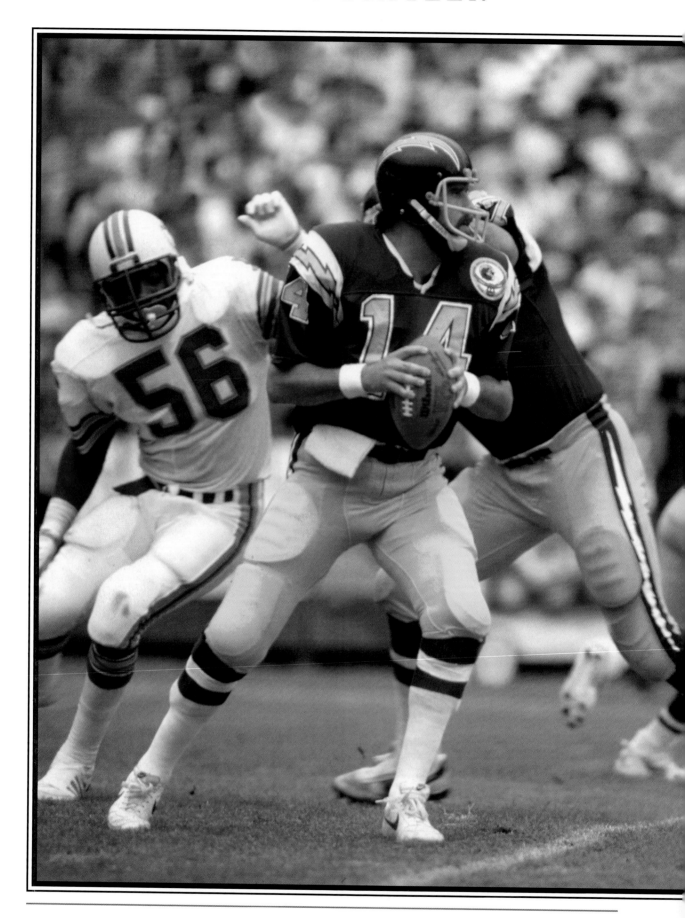

traded to Green Bay before the 1981 season, were Pro Bowl picks. So were tackle Russ Washington and guards Doug Wilkerson and Ed White.

Air Coryell's most dazzling act was a 41-38 overtime victory over the Dolphins at Miami in the 1981 playoffs. It was so hot that Winslow collapsed in the locker room after catching 13 passes. But no Charger was hotter than Fouts, who completed 33 of 53 passes for 433 yards and three touchdowns.

The Chargers took a 24-0 lead and appeared booked for the AFC championship game. But Don Strock relieved David Woodley and threw for 397 yards and four touchdowns to put the Dolphins ahead 38-31 early in the fourth quarter. Fouts led an 82-yard drive that ended with a nine-yard touchdown pass to Brooks that tied the score with 58 seconds left in regulation. After both teams missed field goal attempts in overtime, Fouts hit Joiner for 39 yards, setting up Rolf Benirschke's 29-yard kick after 13:52.

"That game's obviously high on the list because everybody remembers it and talks about it," Fouts recalled. "Any time we

Dan Fouts stayed in the pocket as long as it took for him to find an open receiver. He hangs tough in a 34-28 overtime win over the Miami Dolphins at San Diego in 1984 as linebacker Charles Bowser (56) tries to apply pressure.
Tony Duffy/Getty Images

scored 40 points or more was a memorable game and we did it a number of times. That was always one of our offensive goals.

"I could tell, shortly after the first or second series, that we were going to have a good game, and many times I'd just mention in the huddle, 'We're going to get 40 or 50 today, let's roll.' There was electricity. Everybody kind of expected it and just fed off it."

That playoff win marked one of 21 times Fouts led the Chargers to 40 or more points. But a week later against the Bengals in the AFC championship game, they scored only seven, on a Fouts-to-Winslow pass. It was the coldest day in NFL history, with the temperature in Cincinnati dipping to nine degrees below zero and the wind chill to 59 below. The Bengals won the toss, kicked off and took a 10-0 lead while the Chargers tried to move into a fierce wind.

"Kenny Anderson was awesome that day," Fouts said, referring to the Bengals' quarterback, who completed 14 of 22 passes for 161 yards and two touchdowns in a 27-7 win. "I always admired Kenny. One of his greatest assets was he could throw a spiral all the time. His spiral cut through the wind and mine kind of fluttered and froze. I didn't throw a lot of spirals that day."

That marked the second straight loss for the Chargers in the AFC championship game. They had dead aim on the Super Bowl in January 1981 when the Raiders visited San Diego. Fouts threw for 336 yards and two touchdowns but the Raiders had a more balanced attack and stronger defense and won 34-27.

Fouts was asked before that game if he thought Raiders owner Al Davis, known for his litigious nature and silver and black wardrobe, was sinister. "I think that his tailor is sinister," Fouts replied.

Fouts was elected to the Hall of Fame in his first year of eligibility, though he would have loved to have added a Super Bowl to his dazzling resume.

"No question, that's why you play—to win the big game," he said. "Of course, you wish you could have won a Super Bowl or played in one. But you also have to examine the effort you put forth. I look back and say we tried as hard as we could. We had our shots and our window of opportunity. It's just the way the game goes sometimes."

As a youngster Fouts was a ball boy for the San Francisco 49ers, whose games were broadcast by his father, Bob Fouts. The ball boy became a high school star and was recruited to Oregon by assistant George Seifert, later the 49ers head coach.

The Chargers drafted Fouts in the third round in 1973 and he became their starter when John Unitas, in his final season, struggled the first four games. Fouts was replaced at midseason, however, by Wayne Clark and was in and out of the lineup until Bill Walsh became Tommy Prothro's quarterbacks coach in 1976. Fouts joins Ken Anderson, Joe Montana and Steve Young among Walsh's most distinguished pupils.

"He rebuilt my game fundamentally, as far as proper footwork, reading the defense, timing – all the things you would associate with the Bill Walsh-type offense," Fouts said. "It wasn't the short, dink offense it is today. It was down the field and everything was thrown on time and rhythm. That really gave me the foundation I'd never had."

Walsh described Fouts as "the greatest leader I've ever seen." Walsh left for Stanford after one season, though, and for 1977 the Chargers acquired a new starter, veteran James Harris, from the Los Angeles Rams. Fouts threatened to retire unless he was traded. Then he joined 18 fellow clients of agent Howard Slusher in a lawsuit that challenged the restricted player movement of the NFL collective bargaining agreement.

Fouts testified he would have no chance of reaching the Super Bowl if he was forced to remain with the Chargers, who stood 9-32-1 during his first three seasons. He went back to Oregon during the lawsuit, which ultimately failed, and didn't return to the Chargers until late in the 1977 season. Fouts started the last four games and was seldom out of the lineup the rest of his career.

San Diego and the Chargers came alive when Coryell arrived in 1978. The Chargers finished 9-7, their first winning record in nine years, and Fouts threw for 2,999 yards and 20 touchdowns. The next year he threw for 4,082 yards, an NFL record.

"One of the great assets Don had, he really had no ego," Fouts recalled. "When it came to plays we were going to run, he wasn't so locked in that he wouldn't take suggestions. He asked early on, 'What kinds of things do you like to do and have success with?' I told him I really liked a lot of the things I did when Walsh was there and he incorporated a lot of those things into his style of offense. When you've got a coach who believes in throwing the ball and in experimenting and believes in his players, for a quarterback that's a phenomenal situation."

No coach can take credit for giving Fouts the intelligence and toughness that helped him reach the Hall of Fame. Many lesser quarterbacks had more physical talent.

"You are not going to stop Fouts," said New York Giants coach Ray Perkins. "He has such great vision and timing. He doesn't have a great arm, but he is so smart he could coach their whole offense."

Fouts was slowed during his last five seasons by three shoulder injuries, two concussions and knee, groin and calf injuries. The Chargers went 4-14 without him in those years. No wonder Coryell, who resigned during the 1986 season, once said, "The thing that worried me the most is that Danny has too much toughness for a man who's not as big as the guys who hit him."

Fouts would have been happy to run from tacklers more often if he had some speed. He usually stayed in the pocket while

completing 3,297 of 5,604 passes for 43,040 yards and 254 touchdowns. He was the league MVP in 1982 and made six Pro Bowls.

"The toughness came from the fact I couldn't get out of the way and the smarts came from knowing you can't get out of the way, so you'd better get rid of it and find the guy who's open," Fouts said. "To play the position, you'd better be smart and you'd better be tough because those are big guys hitting you."

Dan Fouts kept throwing to the end. The Chargers lost this game, 31-14, to the Broncos in the last season of Fouts's Hall of Fame career.
Ken Levine/Getty Images

JOE NAMATH

NEW YORK JETS, LOS ANGELES RAMS
YEARS: 1965-1977
HEIGHT: 6' 2" WEIGHT: 200
NUMBER: 12
NICKNAME: BROADWAY JOE
HALL OF FAME: 1985
BORN: MAY 31, 1943

Joe Namath's guarantee was as good as his word and a lot better than his knees.

The New York Jets were 17 1-2 point underdogs to the Baltimore Colts in the Super Bowl in January 1969. American Football League teams were beaten soundly in the first two Super Bowls and that didn't seem to bode well for the Jets.

Namath, fed up with the underdog role, told the audience at a Miami awards banquet three days before the game, "We're going to win Sunday. I guarantee you."

The Jets' 16-7 victory in Miami was the biggest upset in pro football history and gave Namath and his guarantee permanent places in pro football lore. He completed 17 of 28 passes for 206 yards and was voted the game's MVP. It was only fitting that Namath should lead this historic win for the AFL because no other player was as instrumental in the NFL-AFL merger in 1966.

The AFL was short on cash and credibility in New York. The Titans drew poorly, went broke in 1962 and were taken over by the league. The franchise, and probably the league, was saved by Sonny Werblin and four partners, who bought the team for $1 million on March 28, 1963. But the Jets were still losing when the 1965 draft rolled around and Werblin, a top show business agent, told coach Weeb Ewbank the Jets

Joe Namath's roguish good looks added to the immense popularity he earned with his strong arm, quick feet and guarantee that the Jets would win Super Bowl III.

needed a star-quality quarterback. Werblin wanted Jerry Rhome from Tulsa.

The Jets had drafted Rhome in 1964 as a future pick and brought him to New York before the 1965 draft to offer him a contract. "What happened next was a faux pas that may have changed the course of professional football," wrote Chuck Knox and Bill Plaschke in *Hard Knox*, the biography of the NFL head coach who was the Jets' offensive line coach from 1963-1966.

Knox recounts that Werblin soured on Rhome because he jumped into the back seat of a limousine ahead of Werblin's wife. "I don't believe this!" Werblin said. "This...this is not star quality."

Knox already was lobbying Ewbank to pursue Namath, though knee injuries during his senior year at Alabama ruined his mobility. Knox had admired Namath's talent since Namath was a junior high school basketball player and Knox a rival coach in western Pennsylvania. "I could see, even then, that Namath could be a great football player," Knox wrote. "Don't ask how I saw. Man can't explain everything."

Before the 1965 draft, held November 28, 1964, the Jets traded their rights to Rhome to the Houston Oilers for a first-round pick, which the Jets used to select Namath. They still had to outbid the NFL's St. Louis Cardinals and signed Namath to a $427,000 contract on January 2, 1965, the day after he was MVP of a 21-17 loss to Texas in the Orange Bowl.

Namath's signing gave Werblin his star quarterback and the AFL unprecedented credibility. It also triggered a signing war that ended with a merger on June 8, 1966. The leagues agreed to keep their old identities and divisions until 1970.

Namath, under tremendous pressure when he joined the Jets, made his share of rookie mistakes. In his debut, a 14-10 loss to the Kansas City Chiefs in week two, Knox had a talk with the struggling quarterback at halftime.

"Chuck told me not to worry anymore about reading any damn coverages," Namath recalled in *Hard Knox*. "He just told me to go back to throwing the damn ball like I always had. He said, 'Pick a guy and let it fly.' That's all he said. No big strategy. Just throw it. One of the best halftime talks I've ever heard."

Namath was not so receptive to Knox's advice off the field. Ewbank came to Knox one night in Denver, frantically telling him that Namath had missed curfew. Knox sent out equipment manager Bill Hampton to search the bars and when he found Namath, Knox phoned him and told him to come back to the hotel.

Namath replied: "Now, wait a minute, Chuck. If I come in now, it's gonna cost me a five hundred dollar fine. If I come in two hours from now, it's still gonna be five hundred. So what's the use? Why not get my money's worth?"

The Jets soon got their money's worth from Namath. In 1967 they finished 8-5-1 as Namath threw for 4,007 yards and became the only passer ever to top 4,000 yards in a 14-game season. In 1968, he threw for 3,147 yards and led the Jets to an 11-3 record and the AFC title game against the defending-champion Oakland Raiders.

This was a chance for the Jets to avenge a 43-32 loss at Oakland in November in the infamous *Heidi* game. The Jets led 32-29 with 1:05 left when NBC pulled the plug to allow the children's special, *Heidi*, to start on time. The Raiders scored twice in the last 42 seconds and angry fans overwhelmed the NBC switchboard in New York.

The AFC title game turned out differently, even though Namath absorbed a sprained thumb on his throwing hand, a dislocated left ring finger and a concussion just before halftime. He threw 49 times for 266 yards and three touchdowns, the last a six-yard pass to Don Maynard, who made a sliding catch for a 27-23 victory.

Namath didn't throw a touchdown pass in the Super Bowl but played flawlessly and was interception-free, a rare achievement for him. He and running back Matt Snell, who gained 121 yards and scored the Jets' lone touchdown, kept the Colts off balance.

"He can really wing that ball in there," said legendary coach Paul Brown, whose Cincinnati Bengals lost to the Jets in 1968. "He has strength and accuracy and you'd better get to him or he will run you out of the park. He already is in a class by himself."

Namath would never again enjoy a season that rivaled 1968, though in 1969 the Jets again reached the playoffs and lost 13-6 to the Kansas City Chiefs. The real drama surrounding Namath in 1969 unfolded in June.

He tearfully announced his retirement after NFL Commissioner Pete Rozelle told him to sell his share in Bachelors III, an East Side bar where gamblers hung out, or face suspension. Namath changed his mind and gave up the bar. But he still remained a fixture of New York's night life and lived the role of "Broadway Joe."

Namath was a classic playboy star. He wore fur coats, even on the Jets bench when he was sidelined. Though he settled down after retirement, his old reputation surfaced during an ESPN interview in 2003 with Suzy Kolber. Namath slurred his words and twice said he wanted to kiss her. He entered alcohol counseling a month later.

"I like my Johnnie Walker Red and my women blonde," he said during his heyday.

Former Jets teammate Ed Marinaro recalled telling Namath he couldn't believe his idol was about to leave a bar with a woman who wasn't close to a "10."

Namath replied, "Eddie, it's three in the morning and Miss America just ain't coming in."

Namath's nocturnal habits actually were less of a threat to his career than his knees. Though he came to the Jets with knee problems, legendary passer Sammy

Baugh described Namath as "the fastest on his feet I have ever seen." When San Francisco coach Bill Walsh first worked out Joe Montana, he compared his nimble feet to Namath's.

But Namath underwent five knee operations early in his Jets career and his prime was brief. He threw more than five touchdown passes in only three of his last eight seasons, including a swan song with the Los Angeles Rams in 1977.

Namath missed 19 games in 1970 and 1971 because of wrist and knee injuries, then flashed his old form in 1972 and brought the Jets back to .500. He threw for a career-best 496 yards and six touchdowns in a 44-34 win over the Baltimore Colts and threw for 403 yards in a 24-16 loss at Oakland.

"We gave him every coverage we had," future Hall of Fame safety Willie Brown said. "If we had seven defensive backs, we would have used them."

Raiders tackle Bob Brown, a future Hall of Famer, added, "On the sideline, I found myself looking at the game like a fan. Joe was a magician."

Namath's magic was gone by 1976. His last start, against the Bengals, resulted in a

Joe Namath's arrival in New York fueled a heated rivalry between the Jets and Giants. He hands off to Emerson Boozer in a 26-20 preseason victory over the Giants in 1974.

Barton Silverman/New York Times Co./Getty Images

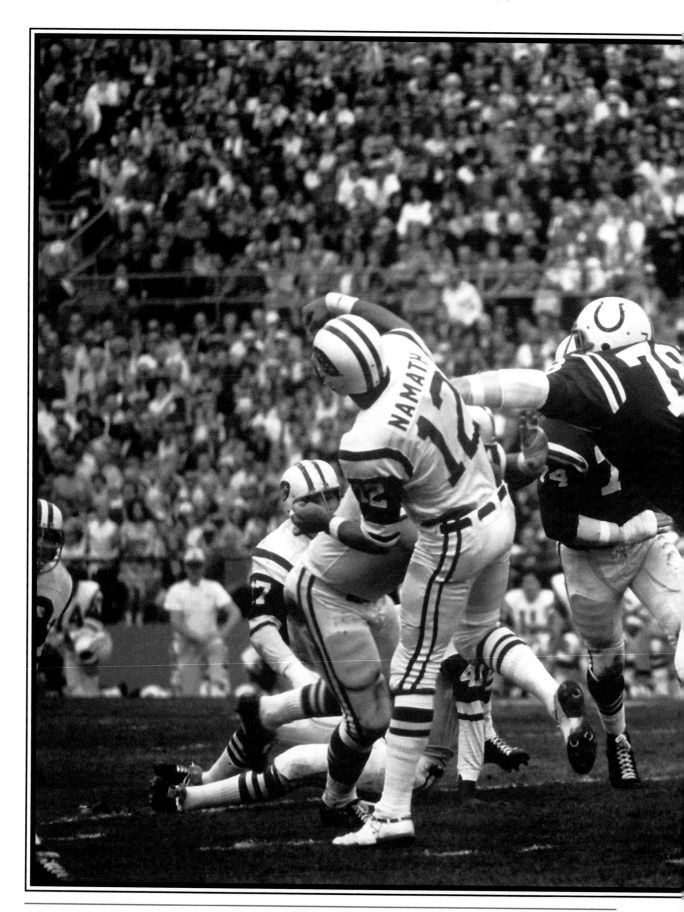

42-3 loss and a 3-11 finish. Namath was granted his release in April 1977 and signed with the Rams, coached by Knox. He completed 1,886 of 3,762 passes for 27,663 yards and 173 touchdowns. Namath, notorious for forcing passes into coverage, totaled 220 interceptions and threw more than 20 touchdown passes in a season only once.

Had he won any other Super Bowl or played in any other city, Namath might not be in the Hall of Fame. But his brilliant play under the brightest lights took a city and a sport by storm.

Joe Namath barely delivers this pass before Baltimore Colts defensive end Bubba Smith can bring him down during the January 1969 Super Bowl. This wasn't Namath's best game but definitely was his most memorable one. The New York Jets' 16-7 victory was the most famous upset in pro football history.
AP/WWP

NORM VAN BROCKLIN

LOS ANGELES RAMS, PHILADELPHIA EAGLES
YEARS: 1949–1960
HEIGHT: 6' WEIGHT: 190
NUMBER: 11
NICKNAME: THE DUTCHMAN
HALL OF FAME: 1971
BORN: MARCH 15, 1926
DIED: MAY 2, 1983

Norm Van Brocklin had a tremendous arm and a tremendous temper.

He set a passing record that has survived more than half a century. He won NFL championships against two of the most famous dynasties of all time.

As a player, Van Brocklin feuded with coaches and browbeat teammates, with considerable success. As a NFL head coach, he feuded with at least one quarterback and browbeat players and reporters, without considerable success.

As a coach, Van Brocklin stood a long way from the Hall of Fame. As a quarterback, he left no doubt he belongs there.

A strong and accurate passer, Van Brocklin enjoyed an historic day in the Los Angeles Rams' 1951 opener against the New York Yankees. He completed 27 of 41 passes for 554 yards and five touchdowns in a 54-14 victory. Van Brocklin usually was platooned with Bob Waterfield, but not this day and set the NFL record for most passing yards in one game.

Houston Oilers quarterback Warren Moon approached the record with 527 yards against the Kansas City Chiefs in 1990. Arizona's Boomer Esiason threw for 522 yards in 1996.

Van Brocklin didn't merely post big numbers. He won championships. He and

Norm Van Brocklin was far from finished when he went to Philadelphia to finish his career. He's getting ready here for the 1959 season, his second as an Eagle. He finished his career in style, helping beat the Green Bay Packers in the 1960 NFL title game.

Waterfield led the Rams to the NFL title in 1951 with a 24-17 victory over the Cleveland Browns that marked the Browns' first failure to win a league title. Van Brocklin led the Philadelphia Eagles to the 1960 NFL title while becoming the first and only quarterback to beat Vince Lombardi's Green Bay Packers in a championship game.

Hall of Fame quarterback Sonny Jurgensen was Van Brocklin's backup for three years in Philadelphia and marveled at his decision making.

"I would stand behind him in practice and watch how he'd call the play and where he'd go with it because I was always a student of the game and worked at it," Jurgensen recalled. "You'd call the same play he called and he'd execute it and you couldn't because of his innate ability to know where to go with the ball."

Van Brocklin impressed Jurgensen even when the Eagles finished 2-9-1 in 1958.

"He'd come off the field and I'd say, 'Why did you call this particular play?'" Jurgensen said. "And he'd say, 'Look, this team's a lot better than we are and we're not going to go the length of the field and we're going to wait until the right time to strike.' He was thinking ahead of the game all the time."

Buck Shaw became the Eagles' coach in 1958 and was able to trade for Van Brocklin, who was upset with Rams coach Sid Gillman's refusal to let him call the plays. The trade was the key to rebuilding the Eagles.

Van Brocklin and his receivers carried the Eagles' attack. They didn't even have a 500-yard rusher when they won the title in 1960 but Van Brocklin threw for 2,471 yards. He also passed for 24 touchdowns, including 13 to Tommy McDonald and five to Pete Retzlaff. The Eagles, 10-2, were two-point favorites over the Packers.

This title game marked the coming-out party for the Lombardi dynasty. But the day belonged to Van Brocklin, two-way star Chuck Bednarik, and the rest of the Eagles. They won 17-13, thanks mainly to a stubborn defense.

A Van Brocklin lateral on the opening play was intercepted at the Eagles' 14-yard line but the defense stopped the Packers on downs. The Packers controlled the line of scrimmage, yet the Eagles led 10-6 after Van Brocklin's 37-yard pass to McDonald.

When the Eagles fell behind 13-10, Ted Dean's 57-yard kickoff return set them up for the winning drive. Dean scored on a five-yard sweep with 5:21 left. The Packers had one last chance when they took over at their 37 with 1:20 left. From the Eagles' 22, fullback Jim Taylor caught a short pass and charged for the end zone. He was stopped by rookie cornerback Bobby Jackson and Bednarik helped finish the play, then sat on Taylor until time expired.

"Nobody ever played quarterback like Van Brocklin played it for the Eagles in

1960," recalled Lions defensive tackle Alex Karras.

Van Brocklin finished his career by completing 1,553 of 2,895 passes for 23,611 yards and 173 touchdowns with 178 interceptions. He got a head start in the NFL when he tipped off the Rams that he was eligible for the 1949 draft after taking enough summer courses to earn his degree from Oregon in three years. He had married his biology lab instructor and was ready to become a bread winner. The Rams pulled a coup by getting Van Brocklin with their fourth pick, the 37th overall.

Van Brocklin didn't play much as a rookie until the final regular-season game, when he threw four touchdown passes in a 53-27 victory over the Washington Redskins. That win gave the Rams a division title, and Van Brocklin played in his first of his five championship games, a 14-0 loss to the Eagles.

Joe Stydahar took over the Rams in 1950 and alternated Van Brocklin and Waterfield, also a future Hall of Famer, from one quarter to the next. In a 65-24 victory over the Detroit Lions, Van Brocklin threw four touchdown passes during a 41-point, third-quarter blitz. That tied a record, which still stands, for most points by one team in a quarter. Van Brocklin in 1950 also won his first of three passing titles, though the Rams lost the championship game, 30-28, to the Browns.

Van Brocklin had another big year in 1951 but his headstrong nature landed him on the bench for a title game rematch with the Browns. When Van Brocklin ignored a running play sent in by Stydahar during the last regular-season game, he was replaced by Waterfield, who then narrowly overtook Van Brocklin to win the passing title. Van Brocklin remained on the bench for the championship game until he was needed to break a 17-17 tie in the fourth quarter. He threw a 73-yard, game-winning pass to Tom Fears.

Van Brocklin never was much of a runner and after he beat the Chicago Bears with four touchdown passes in a 1952 game, coach George Halas snidely said, "Van Brocklin can throw, period. In the full sense of the word, he is not a professional player."

Actually, he was twice a league-leading punter, too.

Van Brocklin, the undisputed starter since Waterfield retired in 1952, threw eight touchdown passes and 15 interceptions in 1955, his first year under Gillman. The Rams reached the title game but Van Brocklin threw six interceptions in a 38-14 loss to the Browns. Gillman in 1956 made Bill Wade his primary starter. Van Brocklin regained his starting job in 1957, then asked Rams general manager Pete Rozelle to trade him.

Defensive back Tom Brookshier, though a friend of Van Brocklin's, recalled the quarterback would not hesitate to harshly criticize any teammate's performance.

"He was Jekyll and Hyde," Jurgensen recalled. "He could be having fun one minute and the next minute he'd be dead serious. If people were cutting up and having too much fun (on the field), he'd say, 'What the hell is going on?' But he was in control. It was part of his leadership."

Van Brocklin's crustiness was more evident when he was a head coach for expansion franchises in Minnesota and Atlanta.

In more than 12 seasons, he had just three winning records and never reached the playoffs.

His differences with Vikings quarterback Fran Tarkenton, whose scrambling style irritated Van Brocklin, were reminiscent of Van Brocklin's tiffs with Rams coaches. The frustration of losing as a coach only fueled his anger.

"No one, not even Lombardi, could chew out a player like Dutch and reduce grown men to tears," said Fears, who became coach of the New Orleans Saints.

Reporters, too, felt Van Brocklin's wrath. Before undergoing brain surgery, he cracked, "I want the brain of a sports writer because I want one that hasn't been used."

Van Brocklin became upset when a reporter asked him if he was still a fighter after a 42-7 loss at Miami in 1974. The coach replied, "Let's stack the furniture. Anybody who's man enough to fight me, stand up."

Van Brocklin, fired the next day, didn't punch any reporters. But right up until his fatal heart attack in 1983, he probably still could have hit any one of them with a pass.

Norm Van Brocklin, left, and Tom Fears celebrate the Los Angeles Rams' 24-17 victory over the Cleveland Browns in the 1951 NFL championship game. The score was tied until Van Brocklin came off the bench and threw a 73-yard touchdown pass to Fears.
AP/WWP

SONNY JURGENSEN

PHILADELPHIA EAGLES, WASHINGTON REDSKINS
YEARS: 1957-1974
HEIGHT: 6' WEIGHT: 203
NUMBER: 9
NICKNAME: JURGY
HALL OF FAME: 1983
BORN: AUGUST 23, 1934

You can usually find Sonny Jurgensen with a cigar in one hand, a Cheshire grin on his face and a twinkle in his eye. You'd never guess how many frustrations and disappointments came along for the ride in his 18-year career.

Jurgensen was the Dan Marino of his time, the best pure passer in pro football but always looking in vain to lead a championship team. While he did play for a few outstanding teams, he never had the chance to take one all the way.

Jurgensen was Norm Van Brocklin's backup when the Philadelphia Eagles defeated the Green Bay Packers in the 1960 NFL championship game. Jurgensen led the Washington Redskins to a 4-1 start in

1972 before he suffered a torn Achilles tendon. He missed the rest of the season, including a 14-7 loss to the unbeaten Miami Dolphins.

"I was on crutches," Jurgensen recalled, "and Don Shula came over and said, 'Sonny, I know how hard you worked to get to this game. It's unfortunate. It would be a better game if you were in it.'"

Redskins George Allen said, upon Jurgensen's retirement, "Never, ever have I seen anyone throw a prettier ball. He may have been the best pure passer in history."

Jurgensen began building that reputation with the Eagles in 1961. He took over after Van Brocklin retired and set NFL records with 3,723 yards and 32 touch-

Sonny Jurgensen, foreground, came to the Washington Redskins training camp in 1969 with a new lease on his football life because of new coach Vince Lombardi. Jurgensen had an outstanding season but Lombardi, sadly, died after that season.

downs. That was the first of five 3,000-yard seasons during a career in which Jurgensen completed 2,433 of 4,262 passes for 32,224 yards and 255 touchdowns.

Statistics are easily eclipsed or forgotten, however, which is why Jurgensen's Hall of Fame induction in 1983 meant so much to him. It meant his legacy was measured by more than whether he led a team to a championship.

"This was the ultimate, to be inducted," said Jurgensen, a long-time member of the Redskins Radio Network. "Everybody says the measure of a quarterback is winning championships and to me a great player is one that really makes everyone around him better. Most of the quarterbacks in the Hall of Fame made their team better. Don't tell me Dan Marino didn't make players around him better because he didn't win championships. He's a great player."

Jurgensen and the Eagles finished just half a game behind the New York Giants in the 1961 Eastern Conference race. "People said, 'This is an inexperienced quarterback with an experienced team and all the pressure's on him,'" Jurgensen recalled. "But we had a big year offensively."

That was the last hurrah for an aging team, though, and the Eagles fell on tough times. When Joe Kuharich took over in 1964, he traded Jurgensen and defensive back Jimmy Carr to the Redskins for quarterback Norm Snead and defensive back Claude Crabb. When the teams met that

October, Jurgensen threw four touchdown passes in a 35-20 Redskins victory.

"I got traded on April Fool's Day," Jurgensen recalled. "I was in a delicatessen in Philadelphia and somebody told me, 'I heard you just got traded.' I had just left the Eagles offices and had a good conversation with Joe Kuharich. It was a shock. Things had been going well for me in Philadelphia, but it turned out to be one of the best things that ever happened to me."

Jurgensen was a popular Eagle with a good-time personality. "When I left Philadelphia, the bartenders all wore black armbands," he joked.

Some friends organized a roast as a sendoff for Jurgensen. "I got a telegram from Red Buttons," he recalled. "He said, 'Goodbye and good riddance.'"

The Redskins were happy to have Jurgensen as he kept chewing up passing yardage, especially in 1967. He threw for 3,747 yards, a NFL record, and 31 touchdowns. But the Redskins didn't have a winning season from 1964-1968 because their defense yielded points more freely than Jurgensen could generate them. The team's signature wins during those years included a 34-31, come-from-behind win in 1965 over the Dallas Cowboys and a 72-41 win in 1966 over the New York Giants.

The Redskins trailed the Cowboys 21-0 before Jurgensen cranked up his arm for 411 yards and three touchdowns and led the biggest comeback in team history. He

Sonny Jurgensen, trying to move the Redskins into the end zone, hands off to rookie fullback Charley Harraway in 1969.

didn't have one of his bigger passing days in the rout of the Giants, though that game set an NFL record for most points scored by both teams. It ended with linebacker Sam Huff calling time out to let the Redskins kick a field goal against the team that traded him.

Jurgensen finally expected a championship was just around the corner when Vince Lombardi, who built the Green Bay Packers' dynasty, took over the Redskins in 1969. Skeptics doubted that Jurgensen, a pudgy free spirit, could fit in with Lombardi's no-nonsense program. Jurgensen proved them wrong.

Thanks to a mutual hunger for success, they got along famously and the Redskins went 7-5-2, their first winning season since 1955. Jurgensen threw for 3,102 yards and 22 touchdowns and Lombardi told a couple of ex-Packer stars, "If we had him in Green Bay, we never would have lost."

Lombardi also said that Packers quarterback Bart Starr was the best he'd ever seen. It's safe to say Lombardi thought highly of both.

"Before Lombardi ever came to Washington, Bart Starr told me, 'With the intense preparation we go through each week, it's a pleasure to play the game because you know exactly what you have to do,'" Jurgensen recalled.

"And that was so alien to the way I had to play my career. The very first practice, he had me call a pass play and I did it twice. He said, 'Look, you're doing it too quickly, give it time to develop. I said, 'You don't understand, with this offensive line, I've got to get rid of it.' He told me, 'Don't worry about it, we'll get you the protection.'"

Jurgensen stopped by Lombardi's office after the 1969 season and was gratified to be told, "I want to congratulate you, young man, for the way you performed and your attitude this year. You completed 62 percent of your passes and you didn't even know the system. Next year you'll complete over 70 percent."

Jurgensen replied, "One question. Look at how many times I got sacked. I thought you told me you were going to get me the best protection I ever had."

Jurgensen, laughing, recalls Lombardi's comeback: "Yeah, but you knew the personnel better than I did."

Lombardi told a banquet audience in June 1970, that "Jurgensen is so important in my plans that if he were to leave, I'd follow him the next morning."

Both coach and quarterback were anticipating a big second season together, but Lombardi was diagnosed with colon cancer and died September 3, 1970. Allen was hired in 1971 and won consistently but wasn't offensive-minded like Lombardi.

"He was going to turn the team around but was going to do it in a different way— 'Let's win 10-7,'" Jurgensen recalled. "He was a genius defensively, but he didn't want us to run Lombardi's offense. It was a good offense and Billy Kilmer was coming in and he knew it, too, after being with (ex-

Lombardi assistant) Tom Fears in New Orleans."

Jurgensen played on four consecutive playoff teams under Allen but often shared time with Kilmer and couldn't stay healthy until his final season. His 1974 highlight was a 20-17, last-minute win over the defending champion Dolphins that Jurgensen describes as "my Super Bowl at RFK (Stadium)."

Jurgensen was mainly a reliever in 1974, yet had a 94.6 rating and earned his third NFL passing title. He was pushing 41, however, and Allen asked him to retire.

"I always felt I could make a contribution, that I should continue to play," Jurgensen said. "I always felt I had the intelligence to know when to get out. But you don't. Nobody does because at that particular time, it was a privilege to play the game. There were only 12 teams early in my career. I don't know that the people playing today appreciate what they have and what it really means."

Skeptics claimed Sonny Jurgensen's fun-loving ways would clash with Vince Lombardi's hard-driving discipline when the famous coach took over the Washington Redskins in 1969. It turned out that Lombardi's offense and style couldn't have fit Jurgensen better.
Bob Peterson/Time Life Pictures/Getty Images

JIM KELLY

20

HOUSTON GAMBLERS, BUFFALO BILLS
YEARS: 1984-1996
HEIGHT: 6' 3" WEIGHT: 225
NUMBER: 12
HALL OF FAME: 2002
BORN: FEBRUARY 14, 1960

Jim Kelly hailed from the cradle of quarterbacks. He grew up in western Pennsylvania, home of fellow Hall of Fame quarterbacks Joe Montana, John Unitas, Dan Marino, Joe Namath and George Blanda. While all carried their talent and toughness wherever they went, none was made to feel closer to home than was Kelly in Buffalo.

"I'm a down-to-earth guy," Kelly said upon arriving in Buffalo. "I'm a guy who knows his roots. I'll always remember where I've been."

Kelly grew up in East Brady, Pennsylvania which isn't a long way from Buffalo in miles or styles. Both have a Steel Belt heritage and take pride in a blue-collar work ethic.

"He had a personality of one of the old-timers," recalled Marv Levy, who coached Kelly and the Bills to four straight Super Bowls. "He came from a blue-collar, tough area in Pennsylvania where people are honest workmen, and he gave you the impression he was here to do an honest day's work. And it spilled over to the other guys.

"He fit in with the Buffalo population. The city loved him and he was great. He was a friendly guy out on the streets. He'd josh with the young kids. He had a quarterback camp in Buffalo. He was always accessible, not one of those standoffish guys at all."

Defeat did not sit well with Buffalo's Jim Kelly, who reveals the sting of a 35-25 loss to the New England Patriots in 1995. He led the Bills into the playoffs for the seventh time.

It did not hurt Kelly's popularity that he helped revive a team that finished 2-14 in 1985. Bill Polian was promoted to general manager after the 1985 season and was instrumental in signing Kelly, who was drafted by the Bills in 1983 but signed with the Houston Gamblers of the United States Football League. He threw for 9,842 yards and 83 touchdowns over two USFL seasons.

Kelly was the third of six quarterbacks picked in the famous first round that also included John Elway and Dan Marino. Quarterbacks from that class accounted for 11 Super Bowl starts—five by Elway, four by Kelly and one each for Marino and Tony Eason.

When Kelly arrived in Buffalo on August 18, 1986, for his first news conference, fans lined his route from the airport to downtown as if he were a visiting dignitary. Buffalo was desperate for a star to lead the Bills back to glory and Kelly delivered.

"We also had (defensive end) Bruce Smith, a great personnel department and total harmony in the organization," Levy said. "You can't put your finger on one thing. But we wouldn't have done it without Jim Kelly, I'll tell you that.

"He had great confidence, which was based on his ability, and it spilled over to his teammates. His demeanor and performance built a lot of confidence within our team. He was physically tough and tough in spirit. He was resilient, a dogged competitor. He loved to play."

Levy saw that resilience as Kelly led his team to four straight AFC titles and never let a Super Bowl loss take the starch out of him. He saw it in a Monday night game against the Bengals in 1991, when Kelly bounced back from three early interceptions to throw for 392 yard and five touchdowns in a 35-16 win.

"That was vintage Jim Kelly," Levy recalled. "Even after the third one, I never saw this look of being crestfallen. He still had this cock-of-the-walk demeanor. He wasn't finished by a long shot."

The Bills reached the AFC championship game in Kelly's third season and lost 21-10 at Cincinnati. They were knocked out of the 1989 playoffs by a 34-30 loss in Cleveland, but that planted the seed with Levy and coordinator Ted Marchibroda for the no-huddle offense. It would help the Bills win their next nine AFC playoff games, including seven with Kelly at quarterback.

The Bills trailed the Browns 34-24 with 6:50 left and went to the no-huddle with Kelly throwing 23 straight passes, including the potential game winner. But it was dropped by Ronnie Harmon in the end zone. Kelly threw for 405 yards and four touchdowns.

"We forgot about it," Levy recalled, "but as we began to get ready for camp, a light went on for all of us: 'Why don't we start with it against Indianapolis (in the regular-season opener) and see what happens?'

"We went down and scored and stayed with it and blew them away (26-10). Then, Monday morning our coaching staff got together and we said, 'This is our feature style of offense.' If it had fallen on its face, we would've backtracked."

After a 30-7 loss at Miami in week two, the Bills won eight straight games and fin- ished 13-3. They scored 428 points, most in Bills history, then in the playoffs defeated the Miami Dolphins 44-34 and the Los Angeles Raiders 51-3. Kelly threw for 24 touchdowns before a knee injury knocked him out of the last two regular-season games. In the playoffs, he threw for 339 yards and three touchdowns against the

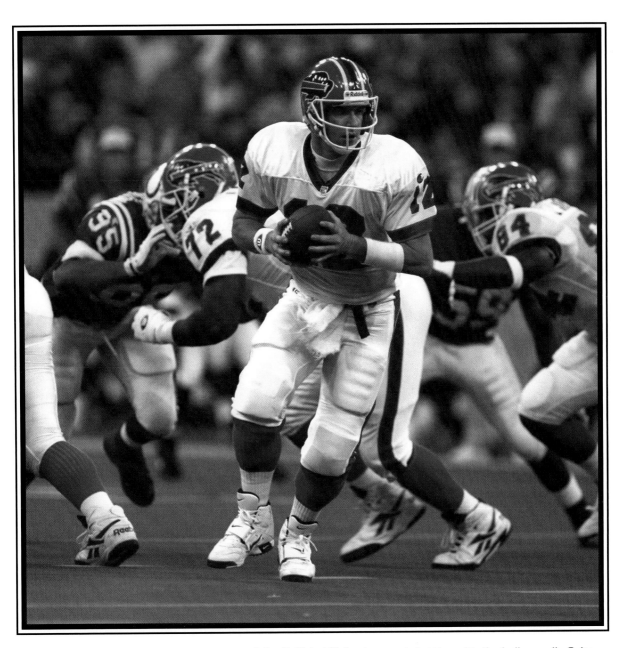

Jim Kelly gets ready to hand off during one of the Buffalo Bills' twice-yearly battles with the Indianapolis Colts.
Andy Lyons/Getty Images

Dolphins and for 300 yards and two touchdowns against the Raiders.

"People didn't prepare for it much," Levy said of the no-huddle offense. "We prepared a package that was very limited because we didn't want to slow it down. We also had a basic grind-it-out package, if and when we got a comfortable lead."

The New York Giants figured out how to stop the no-huddle offense in the January 1991 Super Bowl. They kept it off the field. The Giants held the ball for 40 minutes and 33 seconds and kept Kelly, star running back Thurman Thomas and go-to wide receiver Andre Reed mostly on the sidelines. The Bills got the ball back at their 10 with 2:16 left and Kelly moved them into position for Scott Norwood's 47-yard field goal try. It sailed right with four seconds left.

A year later, the Bills scored 458 points and Kelly passed for 3,844 yards and 33 touchdowns, both career bests. That was his fourth of eight 3,000-yard seasons with the Bills and his fourth of five Pro Bowl seasons.

"Imagine being a quarterback and having your coaching staff allow you to call your own plays," Kelly said. "That doesn't happen. Ted Marchibroda and Marv Levy allowed me to do that. I had full rein of the offense until we got inside the 3-yard line.

"And a lot of times I'd pretend like I didn't see guys running in from the sideline. I would hurry up and get the guys to the line of scrimmage so Marv wouldn't send the big guys in."

The beauty of the no-huddle offense is that it exhausts a defense and limits its ability to change personnel. But it requires a quarterback who can think on his feet and a defense strong enough to withstand long stints on the field.

"I'd say Jim would call 85 percent of the snaps," Levy said. "If he needed a play, Jim would look to the sidelines and point and we'd do it. But that was rare. He had great judgment of what to do next and he was oblivious to his statistics. He could sense the time had come to run the ball and he'd run it. That's one of the things that made our no-huddle go."

Unfortunately for the Bills, they could not make the no-huddle go in a Super Bowl. After the nailbiter against the Giants, the Bills were trounced by the Washington Redskins and twice by the Dallas Cowboys. Kelly threw only two touchdown passes and seven interceptions in his four Super Bowls.

The Bills were heavily criticized for their Super Bowl failures, and in 1993 many critics publicly prayed they would not reach a fourth straight Super Bowl. They would have gotten their wish, except Kelly came through with one of his most clutch performances in a 29-23 playoff win over the Raiders.

The Bills trailed 17-6 late in the first half and 23-22 late in the third quarter and played the fourth quarter without Thomas and tight end Pete Metzelaars, their leading receiver and a key run blocker. Kelly threw for 287 yards and two touchdowns, including a 22-yarder to Billy Brooks to put the Bills in the AFC title game against Montana and the Kansas City Chiefs.

As the Bills were putting the finishing touches on a 30-13 win over the Chiefs, Kelly, on the sideline, mischieviously grinned at a TV camera and said, "We're ba-a-ck."

Kelly's bubbling personality was part of his appeal. He owned a downtown Buffalo bar, which became especially crowded on nights before home games.

"He loved to party, and as a result he had a party at his house after every home game for the entire organization," Levy said. "That built a tremendous

sense of morale within the team. So this is a tremendous guy."

Levy was Kelly's presenter at the Hall of Fame induction ceremonies in 2002. Kelly completed 2,874 of 4,779 NFL passes for 35,467 yards and 237 touchdowns.

"Never mind about his arm," Levy said. "It was great, but what Jim Kelly really had, physically, was his heart. His heart was as stout as a nose tackle's butt."

Jim Kelly starts his third of four straight Super Bowl seasons by leading the Buffalo Bills to a 40-7 victory over the Los Angeles Rams in 1992.
Rick Stewart/Getty Images

Y.A. TITTLE

BALTIMORE COLTS, SAN FRANCISCO 49ERS, NEW YORK GIANTS
YEARS: 1948-1964
HEIGHT: 6' WEIGHT: 200
NUMBER: 14
HALL OF FAME: 1971
BORN: OCTOBER 24, 1926

No other photo of Yelberton Abraham Tittle is so famous. Yet no other photo of him does him less justice.

The shot, a pro football classic, shows blood running down Tittle's face as he kneels on the turf, dazed and without a helmet during his final season. Morris Berman's photo presents a stark portrait of a fallen gladiator and Tittle's bald scalp exaggerates his age and vulnerability.

"The picture made me more famous than all the touchdown passes I threw," Tittle said, chuckling, from his insurance office in Palo Alto, California.

"I wasn't aware they were taking the picture. I was still half conscious. It was the most famous photo of me. It's what everybody remembers. At least I'm still remembered."

Tittle is best remembered for leading the New York Giants to three straight championship games. That was the end of an era in which they reached six championship games in eight years.

The Giants acquired Tittle from the 49ers for second-year guard Lou Cordileone in one of the NFL's most lopsided trades ever. The Giants were entering their first season under coach Allie Sherman and also acquired game-breaking wide receiver Del Shofner from the Los Angeles Rams.

This is one of Y.A. Tittle's most famous, though certainly not finest, moments. He was dazed by a hard hit while throwing a pass at Pittsburgh early in the 1964 season. Tackle Chuck Hinton intercepted Tittle's pass and returned it for a touchdown in the Steelers' 27-24 victory over the Giants. This was Tittle's final season.

"We had some great offensive stars in New York, but I came from a team that also had offensive stars," Tittle recalled. "But we had a long passing threat in Shofner, which I didn't have in San Francisco. That gave us an extra dimension."

The Giants also had a powerful defense, which was absent in San Francisco. Tittle could take the 49ers no closer to a championship game than a 31-27 loss to the Detroit Lions in a playoff for the 1957 Western Conference title. When 49ers coach Red Hickey elected to start John

Y.A. Tittle is involved in a shootout here, a 41-31 victory over the Dallas Cowboys in 1962. He threw for 3,224 yards and 33 touchdowns that season while leading the Giants to their second of three consecutive NFL championship games.

Ralph Morse/Time Life Pictures/Getty Images

Brodie, he traded Tittle, who was going on 35. With quarterback Charlie Conerly near the end of his career, Tittle was a gift for the Giants.

Tittle split time with Conerly in 1961, then threw for 3,224 yards and 33 touchdowns in 1962. He threw for 3,145 yards and 36 touchdowns in 1963 and was voted league MVP.

"People ask me, 'What was my greatest thrill?'" he said. "It was at Yankee Stadium, when I'm standing over center with 14 seconds left to go (in a 7-7 tie with the Cleveland Browns), waiting for the clock to run out. And they're chanting down to the final seconds. It was my first title and a great moment."

That tie allowed the Giants to finish a half game ahead of the Philadelphia Eagles in the 1961 conference race before a 37-0 loss to the Green Bay Packers in the NFL championship game. Tittle's next two title games ended in a 16-7 loss to the Packers and a 14-10 loss to the Chicago Bears.

"Losing three times was a big disappointment because I thought we were better than the teams we played, except for the Packers the first time," Tittle said.

"In '62, we were better but we played on a frozen field. We were really a wide-open passing team with Shofner and Frank Gifford but we couldn't throw. Then in Chicago, the wind chill was below zero. If we played them on a dry field, we would have definitely succeeded in winning."

The Giants were 10-point favorites over the Bears but couldn't keep Tittle healthy. While throwing a 14-yard touchdown pass to Gifford in the first quarter, Tittle was hit across the leg by linebacker Larry Morris, who also made an interception that set up the Bears' first score. A Don Chandler field goal gave the Giants a 10-7 lead but Tittle was nailed again by Morris just before halftime and limped on a painful left knee for the rest of the game.

"I'll never know how Y.A. did it," Gifford recalled. "I'll remember that show of courage long after I have forgotten the score."

The Giants lacked an experienced backup to relieve Tittle and he threw five interceptions. An interception by end Ed O'Bradovich set up the winning touchdown and one in the end zone by safety Richie Petitbon dashed the Giants' last hope.

Tittle had become accustomed to playing hurt. He was a master at running the bootleg, which got him a lot of big plays but also a lot of hard hits. Tittle's bootlegs resulted in a concussion in 1962 and a collapsed lung in the 1963 opener, though he missed only one start.

"Unfortunately, if you play pro football 17 years, you are going to get beat up," Tittle said. "I never broke a leg, thank goodness. But everything else I broke.

"As far as me having courage, we were back in the days when you had two quarterbacks on a team. There were only 28 jobs in the whole world, so you played for the sake that there might not be another place for you to have a job. And you didn't want to give another quarterback a chance to get in and show he was better than you. It's not that I was courageous. I was just afraid another player might be better."

Tittle suffered a concussion and injured his right elbow in a 17-14 win over the Detroit Lions on October 21, 1962, and could not practice for the upcoming game against the unbeaten Washington Redskins.

Tittle told coach Allie Sherman before kickoff that he could play, however, and threw for 505 yards and an NFL record-tying seven touchdowns in a 49-34 victory.

With the score 42-20 in the fourth quarter, Tittle expected to come out, but his coach and teammates wanted him to throw for the record. With the Giants at the Washington 5, Tittle called for a run. Fullback Alex Webster insisted on a pass.

"They'll be expecting a pass and besides, I don't want to show 'em up with a record," Tittle replied.

Gifford chimed in, "If you don't call a pass, Y.A., we're walking off the field."

Tittle relented and hit tight end Joe Walton in the right corner of the end zone.

Y.A. Tittle had a good reason to smile when he joined the New York Giants in 1961. He played in three straight NFL championship games after never getting a taste of post-season play during a distinguished career in San Francisco.

Grey Villet/Time Life Pictures/Getty Images

Tittle totaled 242 touchdown passes for his entire professional career. He completed 2,427 of 4,395 passes for 33,070 yards.

Though Tittle never would have entered the Hall of Fame had it not been for his glory years in New York, he was outstanding in San Francisco. He was the league MVP in 1957 and played with future Hall of Fame backs Joe Perry and Hugh McElhenny and wide receiver R.C. Owens. Tittle and Owens invented the Alley Oop pass, long since adopted by basketball players who lob a pass above the rim to set up a dunk.

"R.C. came to the 49ers in 1957 and it soon became well established that he could jump high and had great hands," Tittle recalled. "In one exhibition game, I was trying to get rid of the ball but couldn't get it out of the end zone and R.C. jumped up in a crowd of about four people and caught it.

"I said, 'That's really something.' He said, 'I can do that every time.' I said, 'If you can do that every time, I'll do it more frequently.' Every time it got to be long yardage and we couldn't come up with a good play, we'd come up with the Alley Oop. We had wonderful success and won about four games with Alley Oop catches in 1957."

Alley Oop was a comic strip caveman and Tittle might as well have been a caveman for all he knew about pro football during his Louisiana State days. After his senior season, he was a first-round draft pick of the Cleveland Browns, who dominated the All-America Football Conference, and of the NFL Detroit Lions. Tittle never played for the Browns, though, and was assigned to Baltimore as part of the upstart league's talent equalization plan.

"In Louisiana papers, there wasn't a lot of pro football news in the '40s and football on television had never come to the front," Tittle recalled. "I was notified by Cleveland I was their first draft choice and they met me, flew me to New York for the championship game (in 1947 against the Yankees) and I signed while I was there. A few months later, I got a telegram telling me I was the first-round draft choice of the Detroit Lions. I didn't even know there were two leagues."

The Colts folded after 1950, their debut season in the NFL, and Tittle was picked up by the 49ers, another former AAFC team. Though a native Texan, he became a fixture in the Bay Area and thought long and hard before reporting to the Giants. He and his wife already were raising three children and he'd established a successful insurance business. Besides, he'd already played 13 professional seasons.

"It was a tough decision," he recalled. "I'm obviously very happy I made it."

Tittle was able to end his career with three glorious chapters. That famous photo of him is nothing but an epilogue.

BOB GRIESE

MIAMI DOLPHINS
YEARS: 1967–1980
HEIGHT: 6' 1" WEIGHT: 190
NUMBER: 12
HALL OF FAME: 1990
BORN: FEBRUARY 3, 1945

During his Hall of Fame induction speech, Bob Griese pointed out that the glasses he wore as the first successful bespectacled pro quarterback had been on display in Canton for a dozen years.

"My son Brian always used to tell me, 'That's about as close as you'll get to the Hall of Fame,'" said Griese, the first quarterback to lead a team to three straight Super Bowls.

Had Brian Griese been proved correct, his father's unselfishness would have been to blame. Griese was so unconcerned with being a star that he was just the fourth member of his offense inducted into the Hall of Fame.

Griese called nearly all the offensive plays during the Dolphins' championship years of the early 1970s. He called mainly for runs and why not? He could call on the powerful Larry Csonka, versatile Jim Kiick or speedy Mercury Morris. Griese also had all-time great wide receiver Paul Warfield whenever he needed a big third-down play.

"He's the only quarterback I've ever coached who down on the goal line, where we sent the plays in, changed a play from a play-action pass to a run," recalled former Dolphin coach Don Shula. "Usually, when they get a play-action pass called, they can't wait to throw it. He checked off and handed it to Csonka and he went into the end zone.

Bob Griese strikes this pose at Miami's 1973 training camp. He would lead the Dolphins to their second straight Super Bowl victory but avoid the major injury that cost him 11 starts during the 17-0 season of 1972.

Bob came off the field with a great grin of satisfaction."

Griese's most memorably unselfish performance came in a 24-7 victory over the Minnesota Vikings in the Super Bowl of January 1974. The Dolphins had 53 rushes, including 33 by Csonka, while Griese completed six of seven passes for 73 yards. Though the winning quarterback was named MVP in five of the previous six Super Bowls, Griese wasn't MVP of either of his back-to-back Super Bowl wins.

Griese hit just enough passes against the Vikings to sustain two 10-play touchdown drives in the first quarter. He then let his running game and defense suffocate the Vikings. This was typical of the Dolphins at their peak, and Griese didn't need to orchestrate a lot of two-minute drills.

"Griese was always playing with a lead," Shula recalled. "That Minnesota Super Bowl was a great example. They had (Fran) Tarkenton and that great offense and they were on the sideline, watching for 40 minutes. When it's happening to you, it's the most frustrating feeling you can have and when you can do it against somebody else, it's the most dominating feeling you can have.

"I've always referred to Griese as 'the thinking man's quarterback.' He spent endless hours in preparation. He called the plays but they were all from the game plan. He would just chart out what he liked on first down, second and long, third and

short, goal line, the green zone—now they call it the red zone. He was meticulous.

"He was the master field general. He knew the opponent's strengths and weaknesses and how to deploy people. He just took so much pride in it."

But Griese took so little credit. "There is no great mystery to quarterbacking," he said. "You move personnel around in various formations, looking for the defense's particular patsy, and then you eat him alive."

Griese's real value to the Dolphins was underlined by the 1972 postseason. He missed the last nine regular-season

The Dallas "Doomsday Defense" was quick to let Bob Griese and the Miami Dolphins know they would have to fight for every yard in the January 1972 Super Bowl. Defensive back Cornell Green leaps to bat a Griese pass in the Cowboys' 24-3 victory.
AP/WWP

games because of a broken leg, and backup Earl Morrall kept the Dolphins undefeated.

But the offense began sputtering in the playoffs. The Dolphins had a close call at home against the Cleveland Browns, a wild-card team. They trailed the Steelers 10-7 in the third quarter of the AFC championship game at Pittsburgh. Shula called for Griese, who showed no signs of rust as he threw 52 yards to Warfield to spark the first of two touchdown drives and a 21-17 victory.

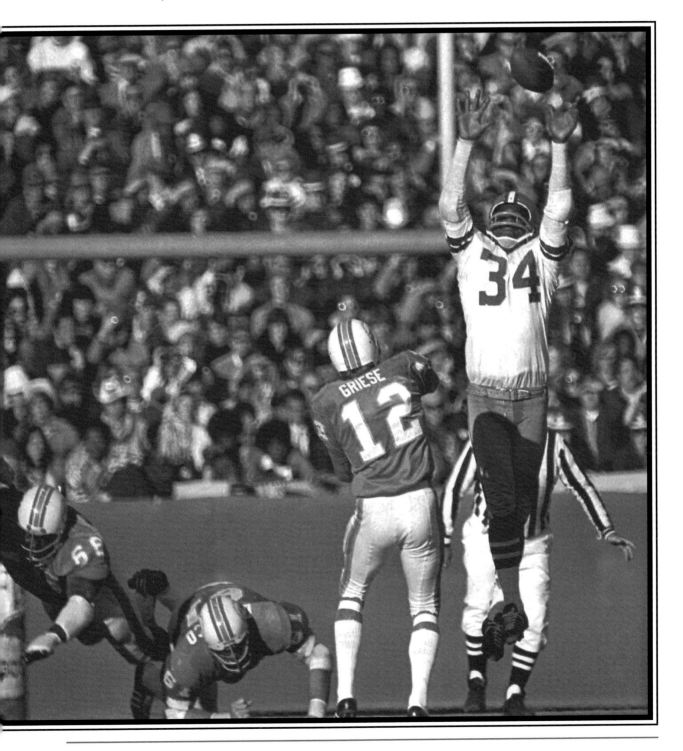

"He started practicing the week before the Pittsburgh game, but I still didn't feel he was ready to start and Earl had done such a magnificent job," Shula recalled. "But when we started struggling, I made the decision to go back to Bob. The toughest decision was who to start in the Super Bowl."

Shula picked Griese and oddsmakers made the Redskins a slim favorite. Griese gave a signature performance—eight-of-11 passing for 88 yards, including 28 yards for a touchdown to Howard Twilley. A 57-yard bomb to Warfield was wiped out by a penalty as the Dolphins enjoyed a win much more lopsided than the 14-7 score suggests.

The Dolphin dynasty ended when Warfield, Kiick and Csonka went to the World Football League after the 1974 season. Griese had to pick up the slack and proved he could throw with the best of them. But he also proved the team was better off when he was depending more on a dominating running game and defense.

The 1977 Dolphins finished 10-4, after their first losing season under Shula, and Griese led the NFL with 22 touchdown passes. He had his top passing performance ever when he threw six touchdown passes in a 55-14 win over the St. Louis Cardinals on Thanksgiving Day.

"That's the nature of the offense," Griese said, trying to deflect praise for his passing. "When we were going to the running backs, they got most of the credit. Now,

the quarterback's going to have better statistics and he's going to get the attention."

Griese got plenty of attention in 1977 when he began wearing glasses to correct poor vision in his right eye caused by amblyopia. He first tried contact lenses, but they fogged up.

But it was not poor vision that led Griese to line up behind right guard Larry Little in a 1969 preseason game against the Chicago Bears. Griese was intimidated by his first up-close look at growling and menacing middle linebacker Dick Butkus.

"Larry Little must have jumped about six feet in the air when I put my hands underneath him," Griese recalled.

He was the fourth overall pick of the 1967 draft by the Dolphins, a 1966 expansion franchise. It wasn't clear for a few years if Griese would help the team grow around him or get beaten down by too little protection and too many losses. He threw 46 touchdown passes and 50 interceptions through 1969. He threw too many interceptions and heard heavy booing well into 1970, Shula's first season in Miami.

"One of the first discussions I had with him after studying all the films was, 'Bob, we've got to get you to stay in the pocket,'" Shula recalled. He said, 'I've been willing to stay in the pocket. I was just looking for one.'

"He didn't have the strongest arm, but it was strong enough. It was almost a sidearm delivery, but he was accurate. He made big plays in big games. Being the quarterback who led us to back-to-back Super Bowl victories—that's special."

Griese led the NFL with 63 percent accuracy in 1978 and played in his eighth and last postseason All-Star game. He was benched in 1979 in favor of Don Strock but regained his job and led the Dolphins to their eighth division title in nine years.

Griese lost his job to rookie David Woodley at the start of 1980 but came off the bench to lead two straight victories. He started in week five against the Baltimore Colts and absorbed a hard hit in the second half after throwing what would be the last pass of his career. Griese suffered a back and shoul-

der injury that forced him to retire before the 1981 season.

He finished with 1,926 completions in 3,429 attempts for 25,092 yards and 192 touchdowns. Griese also ran 261 times for 994 yards and seven touchdowns.

"Bob has been more important to this franchise than any of us," Dolphins founding owner Joe Robbie said. "He came to us in only our second year of existence when we were struggling for credibility and helped mold us into a championship team."

Dueling 12s—the Cowboys' Roger Staubach and the Dolphins' Bob Griese—were the cover boys as their teams prepared for the Super Bowl in January 1972.

LEN DAWSON

PITTSBURGH STEELERS, CLEVELAND BROWNS,
DALLAS TEXANS, KANSAS CITY CHIEFS
YEARS: 1957-1975
HEIGHT: 6' WEIGHT: 190
NUMBER: 16
NICKNAME: LENNY THE COOL
HALL OF FAME: 1987
BORN: JUNE 20, 1935

Len Dawson wasn't ready when the Green Bay Packers blitzed him in Super Bowl I. He learned from that mistake when the Minnesota Vikings blitzed him in Super Bowl IV and walked away with a win and the MVP trophy.

Dawson led the Dallas Texans and Kansas City Chiefs to the top of the American Football League and the Chiefs became the AFL's first Super Bowl team. They faced the Green Bay Packers, winners of four NFL championship games under Vince Lombardi.

"Everybody was telling us we didn't have a chance," Dawson recalled in the office of his Kansas City home. "It had an effect because we were a pretty young team and so many Chiefs idolized the guys playing across the line. All these guys we'd watched on TV, playing in championship games. We were probably in awe."

That awe wore off by halftime. The Chiefs trailed only 14-10 and Dawson had thrown a seven-yard touchdown pass to Curtis McClinton.

"At halftime, the feeling in the locker room was, 'We can beat these guys,' and we did move the ball," Dawson said. "The interception I threw was the turning point."

On the Chiefs' first second-half possession, Dawson tried a rollout pass on third and five but linebacker Lee Roy Caffey

Len Dawson worked relentlessly to perfect his footwork and ball handling. Here he pivots for a handoff in a 34-24 loss to the Pittsburgh Steelers in 1974, Dawson's next-to-last season.

blitzed and hurried the throw intended for tight end Fred Arbanas. Safety Willie Wood intercepted the ball and returned it to the 5, setting up Elijah Pitts's touchdown run. The Packers pulled away for a 35-10 victory.

"I always thought I'd like another shot at the Packers, that it might've been a dif-

ferent story," Dawson said. "But everybody who loses probably says that."

Dawson never got another Super Bowl shot at the Packers but returned to the Super Bowl three years later with a stronger team. "I know they called us the offense of

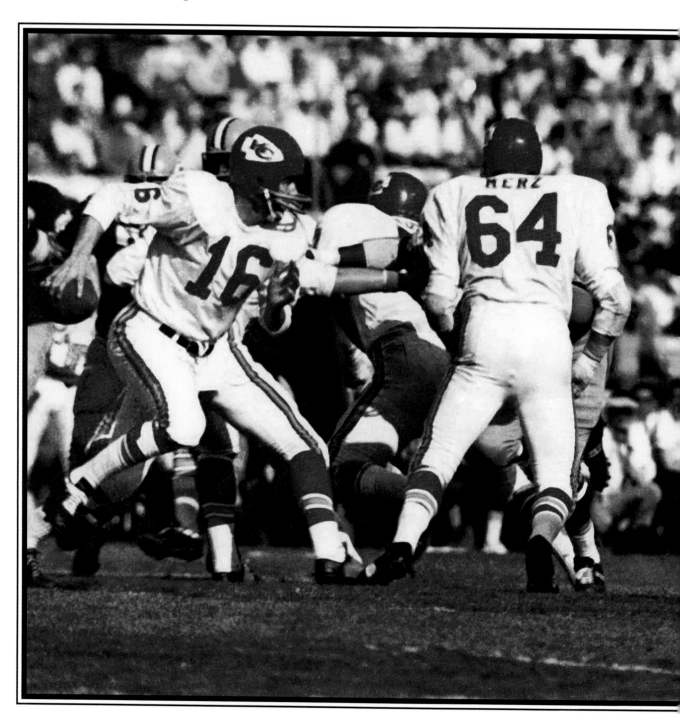

the '70s, but the strength of that team was the defense," he said.

Oddsmakers heavily favored the Vikings, who had outscored regular-season opponents 379-133. "They had run over everybody that year and nobody could score on them," Dawson recalled.

The Chiefs led 16-7 in the third quarter. Dawson, under a blitz, hit wide receiver Otis Taylor with a hitch pass that became a 46-yard touchdown play when cornerback Earsell Mackbee missed the tackle. The Chiefs won 23-7.

Len Dawson tries to avoid Green Bay pressure while guard Curt Merz (64) blocks and Green Bay tackle Ron Kostelnik, far right, comes to contain Dawson. The Packers kept the heat on Dawson during their 35-10 victory over the Chiefs in the inaugural Super Bowl.
AP/WWP

"Timing is everything," Dawson reflected. "In the first Super Bowl, the Packers came at me with a blitz and I wasn't ready. But against the Vikings, they had an all-out blitz and we never could have thrown any other pass. We also went with a quick count and they weren't ready when we came to the line of scrimmage. My goodness, we were lucky to make that call at that time."

Dawson learned the importance of timing long before then. For his first five pro seasons, the timing was all bad. Though Dawson was the Pittsburgh Steelers' first-round pick in 1957, he sat for three years behind Earl Morrall, then Bobby Layne. He was traded to Cleveland and sat two more years behind Milt Plum.

"In those days, you didn't change quarterbacks," Dawson recalled. "You only got to play if the other guy got hurt. It so happened I was with organizations where the quarterback never got hurt."

Dawson threw just 45 passes from 1957-61. And he wasn't being groomed for better things.

"I never learned anything about the quarterback position, I never had a quarterback coach," he said. "They couldn't tell you anything about techniques, footwork, all that stuff. Bobby Layne was a great competitor but his fundamentals were terrible. My skills eroded. Paul Brown was a terrific organizational coach, but he didn't know anything about the quarterback position."

Brown gave Dawson his release in 1962 to sign with the Texans. They were coached by Hank Stram, an offensive coach at Purdue while Dawson led the Big Ten in passing and total offense for three straight seasons.

"As soon as he saw me, he could see, 'My god, what happened to this guy?' " Dawson recalled. "That was my savior. I just wanted an opportunity. You can't be a competitor if you don't get a chance to compete."

Stram, indeed, was stunned by Dawson's regression. "If I hadn't known Lenny personally, I might not have signed him," he said.

Stram began rubbing the rust off Dawson and soon saw a semblance of the brilliance he'd once known.

"He brought me back to basics," Dawson recalled. "How do you line up over center? What position are your hips in? How are your knees bent? When you take the snap, what's the first thing you do with the ball? All the time I played for Hank, we would go through quarterback drills. He would time me getting back to the pocket—the whole thing was to hurry everything but the throw. I never saw that with Pittsburgh and Cleveland."

For the Texans' 1962 opener against the Boston Patriots at Dallas, Dawson beat out incumbent Cotton Davidson. With a 42-28 victory, the Texans started a run to their first AFL championship.

"There was one play that helped me gain my confidence and the respect of the team," Dawson said. "It was third and one, a situation where everybody expected a run and I went deep with a pass and completed it. I think that shocked everybody. That was a tremendous boost for me because the guys didn't know me and they must've been wondering, 'What kind of a quarterback are we getting here?'"

They were getting a quarterback who would set NFL records by leading a league in completion percentage eight times, including 1964-1969. Dawson completed 2,136 of 3,741 passes for 28,711 yards and 239 touchdowns. His accuracy was 57.1 percent.

"I was always an accurate passer and I kept getting better receivers as I went along," Dawson said. "I don't know how much you can teach that. It's like a pitcher (throwing strikes). Can you teach that?"

Dawson found a quarterback-friendly coach and a quarterback-friendly league.

"Defenses in the AFL were not as strong as in the NFL and they had coaches who wanted to emphasize offense," Dawson recalled. "Sid Gillman (with the Chargers) and Hank wanted to put the ball in the air. Everybody was trying to prove themselves in that league. The NFL wanted to kill it before it got started."

But the AFL survived a few rocky years, thanks to a change of ownership in New York and timely franchise moves. The Texans moved to Kansas City after winning the 1962 title with a 20-17 victory in double overtime at Houston. That game helped put the AFL on the map and is best remembered for Abner Haynes's mistakenly calling for the Texans to "kick to the clock" when they won the coin toss before the first overtime. That made them kick into a strong wind.

"Fortunately for him, it turned out well because we had the wind to our back when the winning field goal was kicked by Tommy Brooker," Dawson said, referring to a 25-yarder after 77 minutes, 54 seconds. That would remain pro football's longest game until the Chiefs' 27-24 loss to the Miami Dolphins 19 years later. Dawson never have has completely gotten over the heartbreak of that loss.

"It gnaws at me," he said. "Because I felt we were a better football team than they were at the time."

Dawson still can recite every blown Christmas Day opportunity, most notably three missed field goals. The Dolphins won on Garo Yepremian's 37-yard field goal after 82 minutes, 40 seconds.

"That's one of those deals, ifs and buts," Dawson said. "I thought we could've matched up well against the Dallas Cowboys in the Super Bowl."

That playoff loss might not gnaw at Dawson so much had the Chiefs made another Super Bowl visit. But that marked the end of their glory days and Dawson retired four years later, at age 40. During 19 seasons, his only major injury was a knee strain that caused him to miss six starts in 1969.

"It's not that I wasn't hit," he said. "I guess I wasn't hit at an angle where a lot of damage could be done. I never could run over everybody, so I had to make sure they never got a clear shot at me."

Dawson's 1987 Hall of Fame induction hit close to home. He grew up in Alliance, Ohio, about 20 miles from Canton.

"People ask me if, when I was young, I ever dreamed about being in the Pro Football Hall of Fame," Dawson said, smiling. "When I was young, there was no Pro Football Hall of Fame."

KEN STABLER

OAKLAND RAIDERS, HOUSTON OILERS, NEW ORLEANS SAINTS
YEARS: 1970-1984
HEIGHT: 6' 3" WEIGHT: 215
NUMBER: 12
NICKNAME: SNAKE
BORN: DECEMBER 25, 1945

It was one of the most improbable touchdown passes ever thrown, in one of the most dramatic playoff games ever played, and it captured the grit and slipperiness of the man called "Snake." Though Ken Stabler would lead the Raiders to a Super Bowl victory two years later, he never threw another pass as memorable as the one that beat the Miami Dolphins in the 1974 playoffs.

The Dolphins led 26-21 with 2:08 left when Stabler started a 68-yard drive climaxed by an eight-yard pass to halfback Clarence Davis with 26 seconds left. Defensive end Vern Den Herder had his hands on Stabler, who was out of timeouts

and forced a wobbly pass for the end zone as he fell forward. Davis was covered by three defenders but outwrestled them for Stabler's fourth touchdown pass of the game.

Stabler in his biography, *Snake*, recalled he had plenty of time to throw on that play but his wide receivers and tight end, who'd flooded the right side, were covered.

"I moved to the left to avoid pressure," he wrote. "Just as I felt someone hit me from behind at the ankles, I saw Clarence Davis run into the end zone. ...The guy with bad hands won the wrestling match for the ball and the game."

For Oakland Raiders fans, Ken Stabler seemed an odd sight in any other uniform. He goes to the air for the New Orleans Saints, with whom he ended his standout career.
Alvin Chung/Getty Images

Stabler was league MVP in 1974 for throwing 26 touchdown passes and just 12 interceptions while leading the Raiders to a 12-2 record. They were stopped in the AFC championship game by the Pittsburgh Steelers.

If anybody in the huddle told Stabler the play he called wouldn't work, former Raiders coach John Madden recalled, Stabler would reply: "Easy to call, hard to run. Let's go."

Madden, in *One Knee Equals Two Feet*, wrote: "But when Snake called that play, the Raiders ran it. Usually they made it work." Madden recalled Hall of Fame guard Art Shell telling him, "Just the way Snake called it, you'd think, 'Yeah, it'll go.'"

The cover of Stabler's biography, written with Berry Stainback, has a photo of a beat-up Raiders helmet filled with beer cans and ice. It's a picture worth a thousand nights because Stabler was an old-time carousing quarterback who prided himself on being able to throw touchdown passes on a few hours of sleep.

Stabler, a star at Alabama, lasted until the second round of the 1968 draft, partly because NFL teams were leery of left-handed quarterbacks. They were considered erratic. Also a college pitcher, Stabler was a second-round pick of the Houston Astros in 1968.

"I was told dozens of times that I wouldn't make it big in the NFL simply because I threw with the wrong hand," Stabler said. "Major league baseball scouts were always explaining to me that left-handed pitchers were in far greater demand than left-handed quarterbacks. I had to agree with them."

Stabler didn't prove the lefty bashers wrong for several years. He sat out the 1968 season after undergoing left knee surgery. Stabler, with his knee still hurting and his confidence shot, drove out of the Raiders camp in 1969 and phoned from the San Francisco airport to tell the team he was going home.

The Raiders didn't miss Stabler because they had Daryle Lamonica and George Blanda. When Stabler

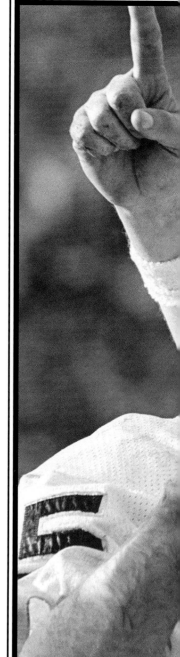

Raiders wide receiver Fred Biletnikoff, left, and Ken Stabler indeed are number one after a 32-14 defeat of the Minnesota Vikings in the January 1977 Super Bowl. Biletnikoff was named MVP after catching four of Stabler's passes for 79 yards.
AP/WWP

returned in 1970, he threw only seven passes and remained a backup two more years. But in the 1972 playoffs against the Steelers, he went in with six minutes left and scrambled 30 yards for a touchdown and a 7-6 lead with 1:13 left.

Stabler would have been a hero were it not for "the immaculate reception," the deflected pass Franco Harris turned into the game-winning touchdown.

"A photo in the papers the next day showed me standing on the sidelines with my head in my hands, revealing just how I

felt," Stabler wrote, "But I decided that for me to run 30 yards for a touchdown against the Steeler defense was a miracle, so I guessed Pittsburgh deserved one too."

When the Raiders started 1-2 in 1973, Madden replaced Lamonica with Stabler. Lamonica was "the Mad Bomber," but the Raiders no longer had the speedy receivers to run under his bombs. Their offense was better suited to the possession passing of Stabler, whose career accuracy was just under 60 percent.

He led the Raiders to a 9-4-1 finish and set an NFL record by completing 14 straight passes in a 34-21 victory over the Baltimore Colts. In the playoffs, the Raiders turned the tables on the Steelers, 33-14. Stabler went 14 for 17 passing and let his runningbacks do the rest.

But the Raiders lost the AFC title game, 27-10, at Miami and were getting the reputation as a team that couldn't win the big one. With AFC championship game losses to the Steelers in 1974 and 1975, that reputation became full blown.

"I wanted to be remembered and I knew the only way that was going to happen was to win the Super Bowl," Stabler wrote. "I was obsessed with winning it all in 1976. The thing that tormented me the most was coming so close four years in a row, and never even getting into the big game."

The 1976 Raiders seemed on the verge of playoff elimination again when they trailed the New England Patriots 21-10 in the fourth quarter. Stabler led a drive that

cut the lead to 21-17 but faced third and long with a minute left. As he released a pass, nose tackle Ray Hamilton's arm hit Stabler's facemask and a controversial roughing-the-passer penalty gave the Raiders a first down. Stabler scored on a one-yard sneak. He threw a clinching touchdown pass to beat the Steelers, 24-7, in the AFC title game.

The Raiders, playing their first Super Bowl in a decade, finally had the chance to win the big one. They defeated the Minnesota Vikings 32-14 as the Raiders' huge offensive line overwhelmed the undersized "Purple People Eaters." Fred Biletnikoff was named MVP after catching four of Stabler's passes for 79 yards.

The Raiders needed more of Stabler's comeback magic to return to the AFC title game in 1977. They trailed the Baltimore Colts 31-28 late in their playoff opener before tight end Dave Casper's acrobatic catch set up a field goal that sent the game into overtime. Stabler ended the game with a 10-yard touchdown pass to Casper at the start of the sixth quarter. But the Raiders lost 20-17 to the Denver Broncos and Stabler's heyday as a Raider was over.

The Raiders finished 9-7 in 1978 and 1979 and Stabler's relationship with owner Al Davis soured. He was traded to the Houston Oilers, coached by Bum Phillips, after the 1979 season but not before leading one of the wildest comebacks ever.

The Raiders trailed the Saints 28-14 at halftime of a Monday night game in

December 1979. Rookie tackle Bruce Davis recalled feeling shell shocked as he sat at his locker when Stabler caught his eye from across the room and winked.

"Snake was just sitting there, puffing on a Marlboro," Davis told Houston sportswriter Dale Robertson. "He looked right at me and said, 'It's all right, kid. We're going to win this one.'"

Stabler soon faced a 35-14 deficit and was woozy from banging his head on the artificial turf. Still, he led three long touchdown drives, then threw an eight-yard touchdown pass to Cliff Branch to complete a 42-35 comeback victory. Stabler finished 1979 with 3,615 yards and 26 touchdown passes, his most productive season ever.

He had an opportunity for revenge against the Raiders when the Oilers faced them in a 1980 wildcard playoff game. But the Raiders won 27-7 on their way to the first

of two Super Bowl wins behind quarterback Jim Plunkett.

Stabler rejoined Phillips at New Orleans in 1982 and, after losing his job to Richard Todd in 1984, retired with 3,793 attempts and 2,270 completions for 27,938 yards and 194 touchdowns. He also threw 222 interceptions.

Stabler's first season with the Saints was interrupted by a 57-day players' strike. When play resumed, Stabler, with a gray beard and pot belly, starred in a 27-17 upset of the Kansas City Chiefs in New Orleans.

Of course, few other quarterbacks had as much practice winning when they weren't in the best of shape.

Ken Stabler enjoys his last victory for the Oakland Raiders as he passes in a 19-14 win over the Cleveland Browns near the end of 1979.

WARREN MOON

EDMONTON ESKIMOS, HOUSTON OILERS, MINNESOTA VIKINGS, SEATTLE SEAHAWKS, KANSAS CITY CHIEFS
YEARS: 1978-2000
HEIGHT: 6' 3" WEIGHT: 218
NUMBER: 1
BORN: NOVEMBER 18, 1956

To understand how Warren Moon coped with rejection by NFL personnel experts, bigotry from many fans and the punishment of 23 seasons as a pro quarterback, it helps to go back to his childhood in Los Angeles. Moon was just eight and going to a gas station to pump air into his bicycle tires when he stared into the infamous Watts riots of 1965.

"I guess it just makes you tougher, it makes you feel like you can deal with a lot when you see that happening," Moon said.

"To have it that close to you, when you see your neighborhood go up in flames, see people looting and see two jeeps with machine guns on the back, pointing at every car and pedestrian that comes by ... it was a real eye-opener."

That was the first of many eye-openers for Moon. In addition to playing football's most pressure-filled position, he had to confront the additional cynicism and antagonism directed at a black quarterback. Moon had a lot more than an offense to carry.

He was voted MVP of the 1978 Rose Bowl after leading Washington to a 27-20 victory over Michigan. Moon would go on to set an all-time professional record by throwing for 70,553 yards, including 49,325 in the NFL. Yet, he wasn't even invited to the NFL's annual scouting combine for draft prospects.

Warren Moon was as instrumental as any player in debunking negative myths about black quarterbacks. He made his point through his success, leadership and longevity.

"I wasn't given any individual work-outs," Moon recalled. "I was the Pacific 8 Player of the Year, the Rose Bowl MVP, had a pretty good season, and I think I at least deserved a look. Some teams were going to pick me lower in the draft, but they were threatening to change my position. I heard it was my size...they didn't think I came out of a pro-style offense...I didn't have the arm strength. All those things were totally ridiculous.

"Of course, they've got to make excuses. They can't blatantly say the reasons why. I knew exactly what it was."

While quarterback no longer was a whites-only position in the NFL, the black prospect had to be almost perfect. Tampa Bay made history in 1978 by drafting Doug Williams, a big, strong-armed black passer from Grambling, with the first overall pick. Moon, however, was dismissed as a scrambler and before the NFL draft he opted to play for Edmonton of the Canadian Football League.

He helped the Eskimos gain six straight playoff berths and five straight Grey Cup championships, though he did not start full time until 1982. He increased his passing yardage each year and enjoyed 5,000-yard seasons in 1982 and 1983.

"It was a great experience for me—a new country, a different environment," Moon recalled. "People opened their arms up to me in Edmonton. I felt I was judged only as a football player. Every time I went out, I was really relaxed. Any time I played well, I was cheered and if I played poorly, I was booed. I never heard any racial slurs, and in my own country I did."

Moon heard slurs while he struggled his first two seasons starting for Washington. His future wife, Felicia, and friends sat in the stands and heard even more of them.

"My best friends got into verbal and sometimes physical confrontations up there," Moon recalled. "They kept from me some of the things that were said. They figured I was dealing with enough—the booing in the stadium, the (criticism on) talk shows, the pressure the coaches were getting to make a change."

After a six-year respite from bigotry, Moon was tempted to stay in Edmonton.

But once his contract expired, several NFL teams pursued him. He was a free agent, then a rare opportunity for a blue-chip player.

"Having the success I had, at one point I thought I'd play my whole career up there," Moon said. "But I wanted to challenge myself a little more. In the back of my mind, I wanted to see where I stood against the best players on earth."

Moon signed with the Houston Oilers, who were rebuilding under former Edmonton coach Hugh Campbell. Moon as a rookie in 1984 set a club record by passing for 3,338 yards but Campbell was fired late in the 1985 season. Jerry Glanville took over and in 1987 coached the Oilers to their first of seven straight playoff appearances.

Moon held the keys to two passer-friendly offensive machines—Glanville's red gun and the run and shoot, brought in by Jack Pardee in 1990. In the run and shoot, which featured four wide receivers, Moon passed for 4,689 yards and 33 touchdowns in 1990 and 4,690 yards and 23 touchdowns in 1991.

"You're really going off what the defense does and do just the opposite," Moon explained. "If the quarterback and receivers see the same things, the defense should never be right. If they're playing outside, the receiver breaks inside. If they're playing you inside, you break outside. It was very hard for people to stop."

Moon torched the Chiefs for 527 yards, second most ever in an NFL game, in a 27-10 victory at Kansas City on December 16, 1990. He completed 27 of 45 passes against a tough defense, led by NFL sack leader Derrick Thomas.

Moon's performance moved Sid Gillman, father of the modern passing game, to tell Houston sportswriter John McClain: "That's absolutely the greatest exhibition I've ever seen a quarterback have. If I were starting a team today, I'd take Moon. People talk about Joe Montana. Montana's a great quarterback, there's no question about that, but he doesn't throw the balls this guy throws. Moon throws ins, outs, up, corners, posts—you name it and he can throw it."

Chiefs coach Marty Schottenheimer called Moon's performance "the singularly finest I've ever seen by a quarterback." He tried to neutralize Moon with every ploy imaginable, even with a mind game before kickoff. Moon recalls Schottenheimer bumped him in the back during warm ups, then walked away without turning around.

"I thought it was a joke at first, I kept waiting for him to say something," Moon recalled. "Then (offensive coordinator) Kevin Gilbride came over and said, 'Did you see what he just did?' I said, 'I'll make him pay today,' and basically that's how we approached it. Just that itty-bitty bump gave me that extra emotion.

"We really were a little nervous coming in because they had a good defense and one of the better secondaries. It was a misty, rainy day and people said the offense didn't work well in bad weather. But we came in and rose to the challenge."

Yet, Moon's performance wasn't good enough for some critics, because late in the game he chose not to chase Norm Van Brocklin's record of 554 yards.

"I had hurt my arm in that ballgame and there was no use to keep throwing the ball," he recalled. "I felt this was a team we might play in the playoffs and I didn't want to do anything to give them bulletin board material. I kind of knew how close I was to the record but I figured I'd get a chance to do that again.

"We have a few black newspapers in Houston. Some people called me 'Uncle Tom' for not going after the record, that it was something I should've done for black people."

Now, Moon was being attacked in Houston from both sides. He was again a target of racial slurs from whites, particularly during a Monday night home loss in 1991. The Moons' young children, who sat with their mother, heard the slurs, too.

"I had to explain to my young kids what they were saying and why they were saying some of those things," Moon recalled. "I had dealt with it when I was 18 or 19 years old, so it wasn't difficult for me. But for them, it was difficult. They were much younger and hadn't been through it. That was the toughest part for me, to explain it to them in a way that made sense. Even some of the good comments were funny but racist, like, 'Hey, Moon, throw the ball like you throw a watermelon.' It wasn't meant to be mean, but it definitely had racial overtones.

"I had death threats in some stadiums. Security people would come over and say, 'Warren, just come walk with us and we'll explain everything later.' Then you're asked, 'If you get any threats, do you want to know before or afterwards?' I just looked at it as people trying to intimidate me and throw me off my game. To kill somebody over a football game? I don't think so."

Moon also felt some public wrath because of his 3-6 record in playoff starts for the Oilers. Though the run and shoot was a boon to his career, it lacked a clock-killing running game and almost no lead was safe.

The Oilers were stung by the biggest playoff comeback of all time when the Bills rallied from a 35-3 deficit to beat the Oilers 41-38 in overtime in a wild-card game at Buffalo in January 1993. The year before, the Oilers lost a divisional playoff game at Denver, 26-24, when John Elway led a comeback considered one of his best. It turned Moon's 325-yard, three-touchdown passing performance into a footnote.

The Oilers won 11 straight games in 1993 before facing the Chiefs in a divisional playoff game in Houston. The Oilers led 13-7 early in the fourth quarter before Joe Montana led a 28-20 come-from-behind win. Moon passed for 306 yards and a touchdown but was sacked nine times.

He was watching television the next April when Moon learned he'd been traded to Minnesota for a third- and fourth-round draft choice. He topped 4,000 yards passing each of his first two years in Minnesota and helped the Vikings reach the playoffs in 1994 and 1996.

Moon then spent a two-year homecoming in Seattle, site of his college heroics. He threw for 3,678 yards and 25 touchdowns and earned his ninth Pro Bowl berth in 1997. He went to Kansas City in 1999 as Elvis Grbac's backup and, at age 44, retired after the 2000 season.

Moon completed 3,988 of 6,823 passes for 291 touchdowns and retired among the NFL's top five in every major passing cate-

Warren Moon was considered too much of a scrambler to suit most NFL teams when he came out of Washington in 1978. But he passed for more than 70,000 yards in Canada and the NFL. Here he throws for the Houston Oilers in a 27-21 loss at Denver in 1992.

gory. For his entire pro career, he completed 5,357 of 9,205 passes for 435 touchdowns. A Super Bowl win was all that was missing.

"In one way, I exceeded my expectations and goals," Moon said. "As a player, you want to win a championship on every level. I was able to win one on every level but one. That was the thing that eluded me."

Though Warren Moon wanted to be known for much more than his scrambling, he could run for key yardage when necessary. Moon breaks loose here during the Houston Oilers' 24-20 loss against the New England Patriots in 1991.
Rick Stewart/Getty Images

BLACK QUARTERBACKS

THE

MISSING PAGES

When the top 25 quarterbacks of all time are ranked in a few more decades, this distinguished list won't be quite so white.

The longstanding exclusion of blacks in the NFL did not end until 1946 and quarterback remained an almost all-white position until the 1970s. The myths and prejudices surrounding black quarterbacks in the NFL finally were shattered in the 1999 draft, when five quarterbacks were taken among the top 12 picks and three were black—Donovan McNabb, Akili Smith and Daunte Culpepper.

They equaled the total of black quarterbacks ever picked before in the first round. No longer would a predominantly black league have only one position predominantly white.

Major college programs did not widely use black quarterbacks until the 1970s and those who reached the NFL routinely were assigned other positions. Black quarterbacks, according to old-school thinking, lacked the smarts, leadership and pro-style passing skills for the game's most important position.

"That and, would a white owner who came out of a different time want a black guy to be the focal point of his franchise?" asked Warren Moon. "A guy he could take to the country club and dinners and show him off as his quarterback? Take him around to

Doug Williams is just getting warmed up during the first quarter of the Washington Redskins' 42-10 victory over the Denver Broncos in the January 1988 Super Bowl. Williams was the game's MVP after throwing for 340 yards and five touchdowns and becoming the first black quarterback to win a Super Bowl.

the good old boy network? Are there owners who feel comfortable doing that?"

Moon spent his first six pro seasons in Canada before he was signed as an NFL quarterback. Though he was Pacific 8 Player of the Year and Rose Bowl MVP as a senior at Washington, Moon recalls being told by NFL scouts that he wouldn't be drafted in an early round nor as a quarterback. He said he ran his 40-yard dashes below full speed to discourage scouts from projecting him as a wide receiver or defensive back.

"I would slow down at the tape just so I wouldn't have too good a time," Moon recalled. "They'd always say, 'Run through the tape! Run through the tape!' I knew if I ran somewhere in the 4.6 range, they'd tell me to move."

Moon stood 6-3, weighed more than 210 and would soon prove he had an NFL-quality arm. Yet, he was stereotyped as a scrambler.

"They never criticized Roger Staubach or Fran Tarkenton for doing that, but if we did that, that's all we could do," Moon said. "I always felt black quarterbacks were penalized for being good athletes. We were going to be told to move to another position where our ability could be used, as opposed to using that ability to make you an even better quarterback."

By Moon's senior year, 1978, black quarterbacks had made advances, though slow ones. Marlin Briscoe of the Denver Broncos in 1968 became the first black quarterback to become a full-time starter in the AFL or NFL. James Harris, drafted by Buffalo in 1969, became the first black quarterback to enjoy a lengthy career. He led the Los Angeles Rams to two NFC championship games and was a Pro Bowl MVP.

Tampa Bay in 1978 made Doug Williams, a big, strong pro-style passer, the first overall pick of the NFL draft. That was an historic breakthrough for black quarterbacks, yet the snubbing of Moon suggested the black candidate still had to be perfect.

"John McKay had black quarterbacks at USC," Moon said, referring to the Buccaneers coach. "And they viewed him as a player who could play right away because of his size and pro-style background. Most people probably looked at me as a project."

Williams fit the NFL prototype of a passer who could see over his blockers, stay in the pocket, throw 70 yards and take a beating. "The idea of a Roman Gabriel, 6-3 or 6-4 guys who could throw the ball, that was the standard," long-time NFL assistant Jimmy Raye recalled before the 1999 draft.

Raye was Michigan State's quarterback in 1966 and 1967, led the Spartans to two Big 10 titles and played in the famous 10-10 tie against Notre Dame in 1966. But when Raye reached the NFL, the Philadelphia Eagles made him a defensive back.

"It was a denial of opportunity more than a denial of ability," Raye said. "There wasn't any question I was a prospect. I was as good as anybody in college. I went head to head with (Purdue's) Bob Griese and beat him twice. The time and circumstances in the country dictated it, and the league was that way. The NFL was not in tune to black quarterbacks."

Indianapolis Colts coach Tony Dungy was Minnesota's leading all-time passer when he graduated in 1977 but wasn't drafted. A slim six-footer, he was switched to safety by the Pittsburgh Steelers.

"When I came out, people said I was too short," Dungy said while coaching the Buccaneers. "Then I went over to the Vikings offices and can remember looking Fran Tarkenton right in the eye, and (until 1995) he threw for more yards than anybody else in the history of the league. I said, 'So it can't be because I'm too short.'

"That was easy to do with the black quarterback. Jim McMahon (of the Chicago Bears) could be short, but they'd talk about his intangibles: 'He's a leader.' With the black quarterbacks, that was never said. It was, 'This guy could be a defensive back or a running back.' And he could be."

It's far from certain Dungy or Raye would have succeeded as NFL quarterbacks and even such ultimately successful white prospects as Steve Young and Doug Flutie at first were marked down because of their size or style. But marginal black quarterback prospects seldom even got the chance to fail.

"I thought everybody (in the NFL) was better than me," Dungy said. "But when I got to play against some of these backup guys, it was hard for me to believe I couldn't have done that."

Williams became the first black quarterback to win a Super Bowl when he threw for 340 yards and five touchdowns in the Washington Redskins' 42-10 victory over the Denver Broncos on January 31, 1988. Williams led the Redskins to a Super Bowl record of 35 points in one quarter and was named the game's MVP.

By then, Randall Cunningham was a star in Philadelphia after making the transition from a brilliant runner to an all-around quarterback and Moon had led the Houston Oilers to a playoff berth. Black quarterbacks kept gaining acceptance and Andre Ware in 1990 and Steve McNair in 1995 were first-round picks. And in an era of huge, fast pass rushers who often flush quarterbacks from the pocket, the ability to scramble has become an asset.

As much as Moon appreciates the significance of the 1999 draft, he's even more heartened to see black quarterbacks without a blue-chip label getting to pay their dues.

"Now you're starting to see a lot of black quarterbacks develop," he said. "That, to me, is the biggest thing. You're seeing guys like David Garrard, Anthony Wright and Jarious Jackson given a chance for a few years. Whether they get developed, we don't know. But we wouldn't know if they didn't even get the chance. I didn't see any second- or third-string black quarterbacks."

Moon said several current black quarterbacks have thanked him for making their road less bumpy, though he suggests any quarterback with a big contract these days can expect to take the heat if he doesn't succeed.

"No doubt there's still bigotry and hate out there and it's not going to go away, but I don't think it's as bad as it was," Moon said. "A lot of (black) guys in college were great, great players who didn't even get a sniff. A lot of guys probably had much more talent than me or others who made it into the league.

"Jackie Robinson might not have been the best black baseball player but he had a little bit of everything needed to make that transition (to major league baseball). A lot of people never made it just because of their mental makeup, intestinal fortitude, not being able to survive what they had to go through. I think that happened with some black quarterbacks, too."

James Harris, drafted by the Buffalo Bills in 1969, became an inspiration to young black quarterbacks when he led the Los Angeles Rams to two NFC championship games and was named a Pro Bowl MVP. He's since become a successful front office executive.
AP/WWP

HONORING THE PAST

RK Classic Throwback Helmets

The rebirth of an original. Riddell Kra-Lite full-size helmets are the actual suspension helmets of the '50s and '60s. The flared shell shape, 2-bar face mask, web suspension, rivets, leather pads, and thin decals are all the real thing.

Throwback Mini Helmets

In 2-bar and current style face masks. Specialize in your favorite team, or collect by era.

40 Piece Pocket Size Throwback Helmet Collection

Each helmet is an individual chapter in the story of football.

Coming in 2004 - Riddell Celebrates 75 Years of History.

Web Suspension

Leather Jaw Pads

To Order Call One of These Distributors Or Call: 1.800.211.7115

Casey's Distributing - 800.482.3485 (NE)
Creative Sports Enterprises - 866.785.5733 (FL)
Great Traditions - 800.309.2211 (PA)

JR's Sports Collectibles - 800.843.1354 (CA)
National Sports Distributors - 877.466.6826 (CA)
Sports Images - 781.938.4340 (MA)

The names, symbols, emblems, designs and logos of the National Football League and its member clubs are registered trademarks.

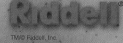

TM/© Riddell, Inc.

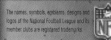